my ikaria

For George and Chrysoula

My Ikaria

How the people from a small
Mediterranean island inspired me to live
a happier, healthier and longer life

SPIRI TSINTZIRAS

NERO

Published by Nero,
an imprint of Schwartz Publishing Pty Ltd
Level 1, 221 Drummond Street
Carlton VIC 3053, Australia
enquiries@blackincbooks.com
www.nerobooks.com

9781863959902 (paperback)
9781743820292 (ebook)

A catalogue record for this
book is available from the
National Library of Australia

Cover photos by George Mifsud
Cover, text design and typesetting design by Tristan Main

contents

My Ikaria

Your Ikaria

Leave home, leave the country, leave the familiar. Only then can routine experience – buying bread, eating vegetables, even saying hello – become new all over again.

Anthony Doerr, Four Seasons in Rome

My Ikaria

Beginning

Some three years ago now, I found myself feeling constantly tired. It wasn't just mental and physical fatigue, but spiritual depletion too. I was stretched thin, constantly trying to find a balance between raising two kids, being a partner, running a household and managing a freelance writing business. My days were full of activity, but I felt like I was running on empty. I was eating too much in order to give myself the energy to keep going – a girl deserves a bit of comfort, doesn't she? – then slumping in front of the telly or lying in my bed each night, totally exhausted. I kept telling myself I had a good life and should be grateful for how fortunate I was. But there was a quiet little voice inside me asking, 'What is it all for?'

We are bombarded with so many contradictory messages about how to keep healthy – eat a miracle superfood, take various vitamins and supplements, use a whizz-bang exercise gadget, or sign up for an experience that will transform our lives. Generally, these 'solutions' involve buying something, giving up something, or stepping out of our lives for hours, days or even weeks. For those of us who are overweight or obese (at last count, nearly two-thirds of Australians), there are many seductive, 'easy' solutions to weight loss – pre-packaged meals delivered to our door, diets galore, and low-fat products on every supermarket shelf. But despite this, Australians are gaining weight at an alarming rate.

Many of the latest fads to improve our health or transform our diets end up being temporary, expensive and token. I started looking for solutions that would fit in with my life, cost little and, most importantly, *be ongoing*.

My quest to lose a little weight, gain energy and have greater fulfilment in life took me from my suburban home in Melbourne to a small Greek island called Ikaria. Having learnt that the inhabitants of the island, particularly its elderly members, outlive people in many developed countries by around ten years, I wanted to know their secret. Why did they seem to live such simple, satisfying and healthy lives? What was it that the Ikarians were doing? And how could I incorporate elements of their lifestyle, diet and outlook into my own existence?

This book is about the lessons I learnt from those rambunctious islanders, and how I adapted them to suit me and my family. It's about how, inspired by the Ikarians, I started doing more of the things that gave me joy and increased my physical and mental energy. What I learnt enabled me to be a better person both in myself and in relation to the people I love.

After travelling across the seas in my search for greater wellbeing, I eventually realised that many of the answers to what I was seeking were quite simple – and *very* close to home.

Spiri Tsintziras

Awakening

She swishes confidently and efficiently towards the consultation room in her dark tights and tan ankle boots. Her gleaming black hair and the swing of her hips in a short black skirt is incongruous with the nondescript sterility of my local medical practice.

My regular doctor isn't available. I've never seen this doctor before. I've just come to collect the results of a blood test, carried out after I complained about feeling chronically tired.

The doctor sits me down and pulls up my details. She doesn't waste time. Iron is a bit low. Vitamin D is also under the normal levels – have I been spending any time in the sun? She suggests some supplements.

She scrolls down the screen on her computer. 'Your blood sugar level is borderline. If it goes up too much more, you'll be at risk of getting type 2 diabetes.'

'Really?' I say defensively. 'I don't eat that many sweets.'

'It's not just about sweets. What about bread?'

'I have a bit of toast in the mornings, sometimes sandwiches for lunch …'

'You need to cut down. I only eat bread when I go out,' she says, her brown eyes warm but firm. She is not going to let me escape with just a script in my hand.

She notes my age, eyes me up and down. At 83 kilograms, I am the heaviest I have ever been. The kilos have crept up, slowly, insidiously, year after year, and they're not looking to stop.

I am just a whisker off being obese for my height. As the doctor talks me through more dietary advice (cut down on alcohol, avoid excessive carbs, don't eat after 8 pm …), I see myself through her eyes – a middle-aged, overweight mother of two who is barely keeping on top of her health.

I fantasise about telling her that if *she* was ferrying two teenage kids around *and* managing a small business *and* trying to find time to stay on top of endless household chores *and*, by some miracle, *also* seeing the inside of a gym occasionally, she too might opt for a generously buttered piece of toast in the mornings as consolation.

If truth be told, I'm just envious. The glossy hair. The slim waist. The best years of her professional and personal life still ahead of her. I'm keenly aware of her youth and vitality, both of which I seem to have misplaced somewhere. I've only forty-four, but my body and spirit feel much older.

Before I slink out of her office, I promise to cut down on bread, get out into the sunshine and eat more red meat. But what I *really* want to tell her is that once upon a time, not all that long ago, I too could rock a short black skirt.

⸺

Back home at my studio office, I lean into the heater and turn towards my to-do list on the whiteboard. *Edit website copy. Follow up on next week's writers' workshop. Finish doing tax.* I read through my emails – a client needs me to make changes to a report I wrote for them last week. I need to pay for a school excursion and more bills. Not on the list are mopping the floor and cleaning the toilet, both well overdue. The minutiae of what needs to be done each day seems endless. Is any of this stuff *really* important? I wonder. I procrastinate by mentally rearranging my work into paying and non-paying projects by due date. The latter list is much longer. Perhaps a snack will help before I get started?

I think about the doctor's words and wander towards the house from my studio to make myself some black tea instead. The winter garden looks as bereft as I feel. The mud-covered lawn is strewn with mottled brown leaves. A ragged line of dandelions lines the path. There are storm clouds looming. I am going to have to pick up the kids from school again today. I feel guilty about making them walk in this weather.

A cup of tea doesn't make my to-do list feel any more manageable. After many months of operating at top speed writing a memoir and balancing several other projects, I'm having trouble focusing on the more mundane tasks of running a sole-operated business as a copywriter – generating new work, reviewing my finances, doing some filing. I give myself one of my many little pep talks: the one that says every job I have ever done has included at least some tedious tasks; how lucky I am to have such a varied, family-friendly job doing what I love – writing. But still, it's no fun doing the tedious tasks alone, without the banter of others at nearby desks or someone to complain to. I suddenly hanker for spontaneous corridor discussions with co-workers. Not for the first time, my workplace feels lonely.

Outside, the rain begins to come down hard. I crank up the heater and begin sorting through papers.

—

In bed later that night, I fossick around in my bedside table for a notepad with the intention of making a list – what I will cut out of my diet, how I can schedule in more gym classes. The blood sugar result has irked me. I am used to the idea of being slightly overweight, but am perturbed by the thought of being obese. I've always had a healthy appetite – and a forgiving metabolism. But my blood results and expanding waistline are tell-tale signs that it's time to act. A list is always a good start.

My hand lands on a journal that has robins, antique maps and stamps adorning the cover. It's hardbound and has a leather strap wound around it. It's a little bit too fancy for a list, but it's the only paper in my bedside drawer so it will have to do.

I stop short at the inscription on the front page, which reads, *Happy birthday Spiri! I hope you have many fun stories to capture in these pages. Remember to massage monthly and keep the writers' pains under control to help you sustain the prolific writing you desire to be doing. Katerina, May 2011.*

My closest friend, Katerina, passed away not that long after she penned these words. Apprehensively, I turn to the first entry, which I wrote to Katerina a month after she died.

Darling heart,

I still don't really believe you are gone. Every time I walk past the photos of you and us on the sideboard, my breath stops for a split second – could it be that you are no longer here? I know you have been preparing for so long. I know that you have been preparing us too – but still, it's hard to wrap my head around it.

The past few weeks I have felt as if I have been one step away from myself, going through the motions of my life – washing, cleaning, getting the kids ready for school. I feel a void, a lack of purpose and direction, and a sense of 'wishing something to happen'. God knows a lot has happened in the past months, but now, perhaps so I don't have to think, I want something 'exciting' to happen...

I close the diary and try to curb the tears that flow. But they refuse to be held back. I sob for my friend, for the fact that her life was so unfairly cut short, but I cry for myself too. I realise that I still feel a bit lost, two years after I wrote this entry.

There is something missing. I look around the cosy confines of the bedroom I share with my husband, the hallway table beyond with its bright vase of flowers, hear the television from the lounge room, and I can't for the life of me think what it might be.

Resisting

The next day, I'm at my desk working when Mum calls.

'How are the kids? George? I've missed you. When are you coming over?'

I realise it's been two weeks since I've seen her and do a quick mental inventory of what I need to do for work. I realise it can probably wait and tell her I'll be over the day after tomorrow.

Mum lives a few suburbs away with my older brother, Dennis. After Dad died some ten years ago, it felt like a blessing that Dennis was living with Mum. It meant that she wouldn't be alone. When it comes to domestic harmony, my brother and mother co-exist happily: splitting the chores, communicating loudly, and keeping each other and the many people that drop in most days company.

When I arrive for lunch two days later, Mum is frying zucchinis on her outdoor stove at the back porch. The aroma makes my mouth water as I walk up the path into the backyard. This is not the time to tell her that I'm trying to watch what I eat. And *all that oil*. But I know what she'll say: 'You can be careful when you're at home. Here, you *eat*.'

Together, we set the zucchini, bread, cheese and some wild greens on the table in the bungalow that overlooks her garden. Outside, the citrus trees are in full bloom, their branches heavy with oranges, lemons, pomelos. Dennis gets the cutlery and plates. I bring the water.

Mum fusses. Is there enough food? What else do I want to eat? I get a little irritable, not for the first time. 'Mum, it's enough. Just sit down.'

While we're eating Mum's delicious food, she asks about the kids. I tell her things seem to be getting busy at school for Dolores, who is only in Year 9 but studies diligently each night. Mum is pleased to hear she received an achievement certificate. Emmanuel, who has just started high school, seems to be settling in and is doing well at soccer.

Mum says, 'They're growing up. May they always do this well. *Ppt. Ppt. Ppt.*' She makes a little spitting motion to ward off any chance that her blessings will attract the evil eye.

I smile and take another serving of zucchini, then ask about her sisters, who she speaks to daily. 'Ach, the same aches and pains, the same problems.' She looks at me as if to say *nothing's changed.*

'Who else have you seen? Tell me some gossip,' I say. Mum's house is always busy, her back bungalow a central meeting point. Neighbours drop in, the phone rings constantly, the kettle is always on. It was the same when we were children. And while it sometimes felt exhausting when I was living at home and craved personal space, now it seems like a happy contrast to my own quiet studio at home.

She fills me in. Her neighbour down the road came by: she is unwell with cancer, has complications with her heart. Another neighbour, who my brother once dubbed 'the witch' because of her long hair and dark eyes, has been diagnosed with dementia, and moved into a residential care home. Mum asks if I heard about the woman with Alzheimer's who got hit by a tram while wandering away from her home in the early hours of the morning? She was a local woman known to several widows who congregate in Mum's bungalow.

Mum shudders. 'I would prefer to die quickly, rather than have dementia. Or a stroke. That would be the worst. Not to be able to look after myself, to be bedridden. I would rather die in my bed in the middle of the night.'

The thought of her passing away makes me teary. 'Don't be silly,' I say. 'You're only seventy-five. And you're very healthy. Don't say things like that.'

When Mum's sisters complain of their ailments, she listens patiently but has no contribution of her own to make. She walks several kilometres each day and keeps a large garden. She isn't on any medication. She socialises. Goes to church. She cooks in bulk, regularly sending us stews and tubs of meatballs as if she was feeding an army, not a family of four. Even though I know that illness and death can strike unexpectedly, I can't imagine anything happening to her anytime soon.

She looks wistful. 'We're getting old, Spiridoula *mou*. Remember when we moved to this house? You were only in high school. I was your age then. Now, many of the people we knew in the neighbourhood have died.

'All that running around when we were younger. Working too hard. Worrying about things. Always looking ahead, when really the best times were happening then and there.

'Remember when we would get together with your aunties, uncles and cousins – eating, dancing, laughing most weekends? Time passes so quickly.' She raises her hand in the air, the trajectory of her life swept into less than a second.

When her hand comes to rest, I notice it is covered in sunspots and dry bits of skin that resist the heavy-duty hand creams I bring her.

'Don't work too hard,' she continues. 'Enjoy your beautiful kids. And bring them over more.'

As I take one last zucchini, I think about the doctor and the swish, swish of her skirt. My stomach is now overfull. Again.

'Don't worry. We'll come over soon,' I assure her. 'But I've got to go now.' I feel guilty, but I must get back to chipping away at my list. 'Your visits are never long enough.' She gets up. 'Oh well. Hold on a second. I've got some food for you to take home.'

—

On Friday night, we have fish and chips as we watch a movie on television – a semi-regular ritual at the end of the working and school week. George and I also share a bottle of wine. Despite the doctor's words, I've once again acquiesced to the children's request to get takeaway; I'm too tired to cook. Dolores and Emmanuel bicker in front of the television – as usual, we can't agree on which movie to watch. We finally decide, and eat with our eyes glued to the set.

After the movie, I stay up late, flicking through Facebook. My friends share photos of fancy restaurant meals, post about birthdays and anniversaries and share memories from a year ago. There are so many people sharing happy snaps of their holidays in warmer climes. How can people afford to go away so often? I wonder.

Before I know it, it's midnight. I have indigestion and my book, which I'd been looking forward to reading, lies unopened.

—

In the morning I lie in bed for as long as possible before the kids are awake. I know that once I get up, the day will begin and I won't allow myself to stop.

When I hear the children stir, I force myself out of bed, and start to tidy the kitchen like an automaton – wipe down the bench, rinse the wine glasses and dishes we left in the sink last night, put a load of washing on. I eye the crumbs on the floor – they can wait until after my first cup of coffee.

My body aches, and I feel heavy with fatigue. It's a tiredness that seems to seep into my bones, threatening to overwhelm me. I can feel my belly push up against my diaphragm as I drink my coffee, willing it to work its magic so I can get on with my day. I regret having so many chips, that extra glass of wine. I'm reminded yet again that my body no longer forgives me trespasses like it did when I was in my teens and twenties. It now takes a few days to shake the sluggishness that comes from my weekend excesses. I can feel a migraine brewing. I stare it down as if it's a recalcitrant toddler, refused lollies in a supermarket and threatening to throw a full-blown tantrum.

As the kids join me at the table, I grumble that they need to do their Saturday chores – empty the dishwasher, the bins and the newspaper pile – before they can flop around on their devices. They look unhappy with my early morning harangue, and I can see Emmanuel squaring his shoulders, readying for an argument. I cast him a don't-mess-with-me-this-morning look. He backs down.

I ask Dolores and Emmanuel if they have homework to do, reminding them we're visiting *Nana* and *Nanou* tomorrow so it's best if they get it out of the way today.

Even before they've had their breakfast, I've bombarded them with other things they need to do. I immediately regret it. Just because *I'm* tired, I don't need to project onto *them*. I take another sip of coffee and watch them slink off to their rooms. I'd be slinking away from me too if I was them.

I'm sick of feeling perpetually fatigued and ever-so-slightly angry. It's not as if I don't know what to do to avoid this feeling. Don't stay up so late. Don't try and stuff so much into each day. Don't have more than one glass of wine in one sitting. Don't eat so much rich food. Don't waste time on social media.

So many 'don'ts'. I can feel myself arc up already, railing against all this deprivation, even before I've deprived myself of a single thing. The minute I tell myself not to do something, I want to do it even more.

I hop into the shower. As the hot water runs over my head and down my back, I think about the things that give me pleasure – wine, hot salty chips, cheesy '80s dance movies. But I'm beginning to realise that all this good stuff, indulged in too often, makes me feel sick. Pleasure feels more like a compulsion, a guilty, adolescent addiction. Something I should have grown out of as an adult.

It's all too much to think about first thing in the morning. I make my way to our bedroom and force myself to make the bed so I don't feel tempted to get back into it. The day has started and there's lots to be done. Who's got time for fatigue when there are crumbs to be swept up off the floor?

—

The next day, we visit my in-laws. They have lived in the same house since they came to Australia from Malta in the mid-'60s. It's on a block that was once market gardens and grassy fields. Over the years, the affordable housing in this outer suburb has attracted new migrants, and my in-laws have seen many waves of different groups settle here and then move on. The rental properties either side of their home are rundown, but their home looks as clean and tidy as the day it was built.

We step into the hall and don slippers on the way to the kitchen. There, the laminate table is groaning with mid-afternoon treats: white bread sandwiches with sliced cheese, fruit cake, chocolate biscuits and *pastizzi* (ricotta-filled Maltese flaky pastries). My mother-in-law has laid out cups for tea, and busies herself in the tiny space. We sit, and the kids quickly help themselves to the food.

At eighty-one, my in-laws are still very independent, despite a growing list of ailments. My mother-in-law looks even more

15

stooped than when we saw her a few weeks ago. She complains of back pain, but still cleans her kitchen floor on hands and knees.

As always, they are glad to see us. After we share the happenings of our week, my father-in-law regales us with stories of his childhood. He describes being a perpetually hungry kid riding his bike around the dusty streets of his suburb, Hamrun. His voice still sad after all this time, he talks about his mother dying when he was a very young boy. And his father marrying a woman who went on to have two more children. He remembers needing to fend for himself, and getting up to all sorts of mischief on his trusty bike. Never having owned a car, he only recently gave up riding a bike around his suburb, carrying bags of shopping in the basket.

The kids listen; Emmanuel taking notes on his phone so he doesn't forget *Nanou*'s stories. My father-in-law is pleased. He loves telling stories, and handing down knowledge.

'*Haya battalia, haya battalia.* Do you know what that means?' he asks them.

Dolores and Emmanuel look sheepish. They know very few words of Maltese and are hardly likely to know this phrase.

'It means life's a battle. So you've got to be strong. You've got to fight the world!' He lets out a whooping laugh as he punches a fist into his hand.

Emmanuel looks a little taken aback, not sure if *Nanou* is joking or not.

'My life has been tough. I was poor in Malta, my mother died. I worked hard in factories all my life here in Australia. But at least now I have my wife, my children, a good daughter-in-law and two beautiful grandchildren. And plenty to eat.

'Here, take more sandwiches. And biscuits. Here in Australia, you don't need to go hungry!'

The kids comply, casting me a guilty look. Here, just as at *Yiayia*'s house, there is no such thing as moderation.

Hankering

Monday morning has come around all too quickly and I'm avoiding the research report I'm supposed to be writing by flicking through random articles on social media. One catches my eye: a *New York Times* article titled 'The island where people forget to die'.

The article has an oversized photo of a man who looks like he's wearing mismatched pyjamas – a blue cotton checked shirt and brown shorts. He's missing two front teeth and squints into the glare of the sun. Behind him is an expanse of blue sky; in the foreground is an untidy field. The photo's caption states that this is Stamatis Moraitis, tending his vineyard and olive grove on the Greek island of Ikaria.

As I read on, I learn that in Ikaria people are ten times more likely to reach the age of ninety than in most other places in Europe. Ikaria's elderly are almost entirely free of dementia and have incredibly low rates of depression. They suffer fewer of the chronic conditions – cardiovascular disease, diabetes and some cancers – that mark the later part of many people's lives in Western countries.

I keep coming back to the photo. Stamatis could easily be my own grandfather tending his vineyard in the south of Greece, or perhaps my Uncle Panayiotis who, well into his eighties, was hunting wild boar and harvesting honey from his many hives in the mountains. I think of my own grandparents, who lived off the land, grazing animals and growing food. There is something about the ease with which Stamatis stands on his land, the natural way that it accommodates him, that makes me want to meet this man and visit the place he calls home. Seeing this photo makes me hanker for my father, who died at sixty-six of motor neuron disease. It makes me sad to think that he too could have still been working his prolific garden, plying his grandchildren with homegrown tomatoes warm from the sun.

I learn that after the First World War, Stamatis migrated to the United States. He married, had children, worked hard and bought a Chevrolet. In 1976, when he was in his sixties, he was diagnosed with terminal cancer. He chose not to have treatment, and returned to his native island to die. It was cheaper that way, and he would be back in the place he still called home.

On Ikaria, Stamatis joined his elderly parents in their tiny house, and took to his bed. His childhood friends visited each day, and they drank the local wine – if he was going to die soon, he might as well die happy. To prepare spiritually for his death, he hobbled up a hill to a nearby chapel where his grandfather was once a priest.

Slowly but surely his energy returned, and he began tending his parents' garden. As he grew stronger, Stamatis built a few extra rooms in the house so that his adult children would have somewhere to stay when they visited.

Nearly thirty years later, when the *New York Times* covered his story, Stamatis was ninety-seven years old and cancer free. Still working in his fields, he boasted of producing 400 gallons of wine each year.

How is it that in my travels to Greece I never heard of Ikaria, 'the island where people forget to die'? I wonder. If Stamatis, who has nearly reached his hundredth year, can look and feel so vital, why can't I, given I'm just half his age? I need to find out more.

I immediately indulge in the cheapest and easiest form of travel to Ikaria – via the internet.

I find that Ikaria is a small island near the west coast of Turkey, an isolated place of windswept pine and oak forests, with little arable land.

According to myth, a young Icarus, imprisoned in a labyrinth, used wax wings to escape. He was warned not to fly too close to the sun, but ignored this advice. The wax on his wings melted and he fell into the sea. Icarus's body was carried ashore to an island as yet unnamed. The divinity Heracles come across the body and, recognising Icarus, buried him on a small rocky outcrop jutting out of the Aegean Sea, calling it Ikaria.

The sea around Ikaria was, even in Homeric times, one of the most turbulent areas of the Aegean. It lacked a natural port where boats could dock, adding to its inaccessibility. But its isolation didn't stop invaders. Persians, Romans and Turks all laid siege to Ikaria at some time or another and it was under constant threat from pirates. Allegedly, it was the fear of pirates that forced the islanders to move inland and begin to open their shops in the small hours of the morning.

I also learn that Ikaria was reputedly the birthplace of Dionysius, the God of wine, and was renowned for its notable Pramnian wine, possibly in the fourth century BC. The locals still wax lyrical about the quality of their wine, and drink it mixed with water, just as their ancient forebears did. Many edible wild plants grow on the island, and mineral springs spurt from its rocky depths.

I discover that many of the islanders live simply, traditionally, and according to the seasons. They still fortify their houses from the weather and make sure they've preserved enough of their summer produce to tide them over during the barren winter months. They work together, sharing resources and skills. They stride around the harsh mountainous landscape tending their animals and fields. People congregate regularly in village squares, churches and *cafeneions* to celebrate, pray and gossip. Ikaria is nowhere near as flashy as the nearby island of Samos, with its large villas and more obvious tourist attractions, but it appears the locals like it that way.

I have no illusion that the Ikarians' way of living isn't hard – my own grandparents lived in a similar way in small, poor villages in southern Greece. Mum lived in a seaside town, where her parents harvested grapes. Dad lived in the mountains, his family making their way to the fields below each summer to tend their fields of watermelons. They often struggled, with few of the amenities we now take for granted – running water, electricity, telephones. It was those hardships that compelled their children, my parents, to leave their homeland and come to Australia. Here they worked in various manual jobs in factories, making the things that Australia needed at the time – cars and clothes, beer and ammunitions.

Now here I am in my home office – several wires poking out from under my desk connecting me to the outside world and I search the internet in an attempt to feel closer to a people that remind me of my own grandparents, hankering for something I seem to have lost. The irony is not lost on me.

I stop searching and sigh. I need to get back to work on a research report.

——

A few weeks later, I find myself kneeling on the floor, my knees feel cold against the kitchen tiles. My head is placed awkwardly as I poke around in the dishwasher, which has stopped working. The hole where the water is supposed to drain away is blocked. I plunge my hand into the grey water and scoop out bits of pasta, brown sludgy vegetables and a small sliver of broken glass. The water still won't pass through and my fingers slide against slime as I dig deeper to find the source of the blockage.

Dolores leaves a glass on the sink and pulls a face at the glug in my hand, saying, 'That's disgusting.'

I look up at her, annoyed, and she slinks away. Never mess with Mum when she's on her hands and knees. Cleaning the toilet. Wiping cat vomit off floorboards. Scrubbing unidentifiable stains off kitchen tiles.

When we moved into our home, our kitchen had a dishwasher-sized hole, but no dishwasher. The dishwasher I am clearing was a generous gift from my cousin Kathy, who won it in a competition. She knew I wanted one – so she simply gave it to me. It's a godsend and I so appreciate Kathy's kindness, but part of me wonders if the dishwasher has caused more grief than joy, as George and I often find ourselves grumbling to the kids: 'Please put your dishes in the dishwasher!' 'Whose turn is it to empty the dishwasher?' The fact that we no longer have to wash our own dishes is now taken for granted. And our ritual of washing up and drying together at the end of the night has become a thing of the past.

After finally getting enough sludge out of the filter to allow the water to drain slowly away, I feel a fleeting sense of satisfaction.

Not for the first time, I consider the futility of cleaning. It's nearly impossible to keep on top of the dust that collects on furniture; the hairs that collect in the drain of the shower and around the toilet base; the cat fluff that gathers so insidiously in corners. Faced with the continual detritus that we seem to create as a family, I often feel my spirits lag. It's like a weight on my shoulders, dragging them down.

—

Later that night, I take myself off to bed and find myself once again entering 'Ikaria' into the search engine. I come across a documentary about the island by Nikos Dyanas, titled *Little Land.* In it the filmmaker introduces an 83-year-old café owner, beekeeper and farmer, Yiorgos Stenos, who says the islanders do many jobs to survive. 'For Ikarians, doing one job equals poverty,' he says. 'If I have no customer, I go to my bees for honey. If there's no honey, I make some olive oil. No oil, I plant some vegetables. That's how I make the most of my waking hours. We work slowly, steadily and every day. Work tires us physically, but not mentally, so we feel great because we like what we do.'

In another interview, 101-year-old Ikarian resident weaver and teacher Ioanna Prois says, 'We didn't have much to eat when I was a girl. Mostly *horta* (wild greens). I have always worked and I get great satisfaction from my loom, from creating. I always wake up positive and I never give up hope and I don't eat very much. I have energy. Lots of it. If I could do a mountain of work, I would! Life is beautiful, but only if we can live it well. Life must be enjoyed.'

The overarching message from the islanders is that the secret to living well is not about having what you want, but having what you need – and being content with 'enough'.

As the documentary credits roll, an idea takes hold. I imagine myself walking beside Yiorgos as he collects honey from his bees and sitting next to Ioanna learning how to weave as she tells me about her childhood. For the first time in a long time, I feel excited. Perhaps a trip to Ikaria is what I have been looking for.

I feel a naughty thrill as I enter 'Ikaria accommodation' into my search engine. I expect to find very little, perhaps some rustic village homes, but it seems there are a good number of hotels and studios with glimmering pools overlooking the particular shade of Mediterranean blue that makes my heart sing. The views are impossibly beautiful. I daydream about the trips I've made to the Greek islands over the years – dancing at a seaside resort in Mykonos with my friend Stacey, walking the Samaria Gorge with family friends in Crete, eating at a charming seaside taverna in Ithaka with George and the kids several years ago ...

I whittle away the better part of an hour entering dates for flights into search engines. But when I mentally tally the cost of going with the whole family, or, conversely, the cost of going by myself and leaving the family and my work behind, I give up. Who am I kidding?

Shutting down the fun windows, I start a more serious search, entering, 'Why do Ikarians live so long?'

A list of international articles from the *Guardian*, the *New York Times* and CNN-online come up. From these I learn that the Ikarians don't *try* to live for a long time – it just happens. They are not on complex treatments or programs. They don't have a regimented diet that allows them to eat some things and not others, nor do they have vexed and guilty relationships with food. It doesn't look like there is a single 'superfood' that keeps them healthy. They don't use gyms, fiddly tracking devices and other gadgetry to help them keep fit. Expensive or complicated ways of relaxing or notions of 'getting away from it all' are unheard of. It's all refreshingly simple – it appears that their everyday routines make for a long life, and in a way that ensures they are healthy, happy and active for most of their lives.

I dig a bit deeper and find several research papers by notable Greek doctors and academics. Everything they say makes complete sense to me. The Ikarians live almost exactly as my grandparents did – and, to a degree, how my parents lived when we were growing up, even when they came to suburban Melbourne. Even now, though my mum is in her mid-seventies, she still keeps active in her garden, socialises lots, walks a few kilometres to pick something up from the shop.

The Ikarians are frequently on the move during their day. They don't go out of their way to exercise. Their environment just encourages them to be active. They walk up and down mountainsides, tend their fields, do their housework and dance at their many village feasts. I read that six out of ten Ikarians over the age of ninety are still physically active. Public health studies show that even moderate walking lowers cholesterol and blood pressure, and can reduce everything from stress to the risk of diabetes, vascular stiffness and inflammation, dementia and depression.

Elderly Ikarians largely follow a traditional Mediterranean diet. I am reminded of the principles of such a diet when I pull from my bookshelves *The Mediterranean Diet Cookbook* by Dr Catherine Itsiopoulos. A respected Melbourne academic and author on Mediterranean food, she writes that the Mediterranean diet has been around for several millennia, and is one of the most comprehensively researched and scientifically validated diets in human history. She notes that thousands of studies have demonstrated that the traditional Mediterranean diet reduces chronic disease and mortality, including incidence of cardiovascular disease, cancer, and neurodegenerative diseases such as Alzheimer's and Parkinson's. The beauty of the Mediterranean diet is that it focuses on what you *can* eat, rather than what you can't. She also emphasises its value beyond just food, citing a UNESCO committee statement: 'The Mediterranean diet emphasizes values of hospitality, neighbourliness, intercultural dialogue and creativity, and a way of life guided by respect for diversity.'

Back at my computer, another research article reminds me of what I have already learnt from my grandparents: that while the traditional Mediterranean diet varies across the countries where it is practised, it is generally high in vegetables, fruits, nuts, legumes, grains and olive oil, with moderate amounts of fish. It is low in dairy products, red meat and poultry. Alcohol, especially wine with meals, is drunk regularly but in moderation. I delve further and find that Ikarian cookbook author Diane Kochilas talks about how the diet of the island's elders comprised a few basics, with foraged foods, especially greens, providing a solid foundation. She notes that it wasn't so much *what* elders ate, but *how little of it* they ate that kept them healthy.

It appears that the Ikarians diverge from the traditional Mediterranean diet in that they eat larger amounts of potatoes. The elders there grew up eating red meat very sparingly. They drink goat's milk and eat cheese in moderation. Their main fat comes from extra virgin olive oil, which they use generously in cooking and on salads. They use herbs to flavour food and make teas, and have access to many wild foods on the island. The traditional Ikarian diet includes very little processed food, and is based on what is seasonally available, or what has been preserved from gardens and fields. Ikarians have traditionally fasted for up to half of the year, refraining from eating meat and dairy products. This cuts around 30 per cent of calories out of their diet. Though fast food has made some inroads into the island, the basis of their diet is still fresh, seasonal produce, which is often home-grown and organic.

But the islanders' wellbeing is not just about food. The centre of Ikarian social life is the family, which includes extended family. They enjoy connections with their fellow villagers and those in surrounding villages, of which there are several on the island.

Traditionally in Greece, the *cafeneion* is a village gathering place to talk and argue, play backgammon and drink coffee, particularly for men. It is no different in Ikaria, except that women are just as likely to be rolling the dice as men. There are more than two hundred village feasts and celebrations (*panigiria*) throughout the year that both residents and tourists enthusiastically attend. This is a way of raising money for communal village projects, with the added benefit of celebrating and connecting.

I discover that elderly Ikarians relax and rest by taking short naps during the day. Almost all those studied aged over ninety have a siesta at noon. Some researchers believe that this might explain the very low incidence of depression among elders on the island. A midday siesta may lower a person's risk of death from heart disease, possibly by reducing stress levels.

Ikarians mostly drink water. A lot of families produce their own wine, which they water down and drink moderately with meals, usually in company. They also mostly drink Turkish-style black coffee, and tea brewed from local herbs. I think back to research I've read showing that coffee drinkers have a lower risk of getting type 2 diabetes and heart attacks. The Ikarians tick all the boxes for healthy living, seemingly without trying.

While the Ikarians no doubt get stressed like the rest of us, research shows that their lifestyle and habits help reduce it – moving lots, socialising, eating whole foods, getting out in the sun. While it's hard to measure stress, studies have shown that prolonged stress is linked with many health problems, including a higher risk of getting cardiovascular disease, higher levels of 'bad' cholesterol and lower levels of 'good' cholesterol, and our cells becoming inflamed.

The more I read, the more enamoured I become with the island and its people. What the Ikarians do sounds so simple, cutting through the many complicated messages we receive in the West about how we can be happier and healthier.

—

It's a Friday and I'm swimming laps with my friend Fiona at our local outdoor pool. Inspired by the doctor's words several weeks ago, I've coerced Fiona into baring her winter skin once a week in the interests of health. There is no one else in our lane, and we swim side by side, debriefing about our week, talking more than exerting. While it's cold, the early morning sun plays on the ripples that push out from our bodies, and I think of all that bone-strengthening Vitamin D my body must be making.

I tell Fiona I have 'discovered' a Greek island and tell her some of what I've learnt about Ikaria, saying how much I'd like to visit it and find out more about what makes the people there live such a long time. We entertain the idea of going on a holiday there together, as if we were still single and childless. As we talk about the food we would eat, I fantasise about wild green pies and goat's milk yoghurt and aromatic honey, the mountain walks we would take, visiting isolated bell towers and whitewashed churches on windy outcrops.

But then Fiona confesses that the idea of travelling doesn't really excite her – with all the preparation, the long claustrophobic plane trip, and then being away from home for so long.

As we soak up the sun, languid stroke by languid stroke, Fiona turns to me and says, 'You should just do it yourself, Spiri.'

Starting

The days and weeks roll on and winter turns into spring. My mood improves perceptibly with the little changes that the sunnier weather heralds: the first blooms in our garden poking up; being able to have the odd meal on the outdoor table under the olive tree; hanging clothes outside, rather than inside, the house.

All my reading about Ikaria over the past months, and this renewed sense of joy from the simple pleasures reminds me of some of the things my own ancestors did – eating largely seasonal, 'real' food, living mindfully, celebrating their lives each day through rituals and rhythms that were guided not just by clocks, but by their natural environment. I reflect that spring is traditionally a time of renewal. And so, one Saturday morning, I decide to bring this ethos into our home by clearing our pantry and fridge of foods that my grandmother might not recognise.

I place all the jars, packets and tins on our kitchen bench. The food stretches along its length. I read the ingredients of my kids' favourite cereal, which runs down the side of the packaging. The second ingredient is sugar. I wonder if the kids will notice the disappearance of these foods. The rice crackers, which I've perceived as a relatively 'healthy' treat compared to potato chips, are made of up seventeen ingredients. One packet has 10 per cent of the daily recommended salt intake. It's not uncommon for me to mindlessly eat the whole packet while watching a movie.

I throw away the more sugary and salty products, and those things that have a massive list of ingredients – they wouldn't pass what I now start to think of as the *yiayia* test. I keep the cereal until we can decide a suitable replacement. Some things stay, despite failing the test – soy sauce, sweet chilli sauce, Vegemite – I tell myself this needs to be a food revolution by stealth, not an outright coup. I decant the grains and nuts into jars so we can see them, perhaps inspiring us to eat them more often; I place the fruits and vegetables in the fridge or in a bowl on the table so that they are within sight. By the time I finish, our kitchen has had a make-over and looks neat and trim. I start a shopping list which includes legumes, grains, nuts and lots of fresh produce. No rice crackers. I put a question mark beside cereal. Somehow, I don't think the kids will accept porridge every morning.

Just as I finish, Katerina's first cousin, Angela, texts. *Just got back from Ikaria. Would love to tell you all about it xx Ang.* Her timing is impeccable.

Since Katerina died, Angela and I have become friends. Seeing each other helps us keep her memory alive. I mentally thank Katerina for fostering so many connections between the people she loved, even after she has gone. I invite Angela to lunch – both to see her, and to find out more about her time in Ikaria.

—

Over our meal, Angela tells me that the Ikarian terrain was rugged and the taxis expensive. The taxi driver who was supposed to take her and her friends from their arrival port to the isolated mountain village where they were staying complained that the group and their luggage wouldn't fit into the one taxi they'd ordered.

'It's not our fault you're too fat – how much do you eat in Australia?' the taxi driver had scoffed, before unapologetically leaving half the group to wait for another taxi, which arrived in its own good time.

When I ask Angela why she chose to visit Ikaria, she shrugs and says, 'To learn what the secret to a long life is.'

'And what is it?' I ask, leaning forward.

She answers by telling me a story about a new resident on the island who asked a local carpenter if he could fix a broken window. The local carpenter agreed and promised to come on Tuesday. When he didn't arrive the following week, the man wandered down to the *cafeneion* and found the carpenter drinking coffee and playing backgammon. When he asked the carpenter why he hadn't come to do the job, the man answered, 'I said I would come on Tuesday. I didn't say which one.' Angela laughs. The Ikarians appear not to worry at all about time, and while she was on the island, she didn't worry about it either.

'I hope that feeling lasts, Angela,' I say, knowing from experience that it's one thing to feel relaxed on a Mediterranean island while you're on holidays, another to sustain that sensation when you return home.

For me, time is a big concern: I'm always trying to squeeze the life out of it and wishing there was more of it. Trying to slow it down as I watch my kids grow up too fast, my body age, my mother get older. Trying to stuff as much as I can into each day, getting to bed later and later, spending too much time on social media, waking in the small hours of the morning, worrying about whether I'm a good enough mother, whether I'm spending enough time with my husband, whether I could be earning more.

As I see Angela out, I realise that one of the main things I *really* want to learn from the Ikarians is how I can make peace with time.

Learning

A few weeks later, the pantry and fridge are still looking nicely 'made-over', as I've gotten into a weekly habit of doing a quick tidy before making a shopping list. Now that there is not so much processed food in the pantry, the kids seem more inclined to choose fruit and whatever is in front of them in the vegetable bowl as a snack. I mentally high five the Ikarians.

I tell the kids that it is commendable that they are making healthy choices. While they agree in principle that it is sensible to eat less processed food, they are hesitant to knock back the many treats that come their way. *Yiayia* comes over with a tube of crisps and they are gone within hours. George still brings home a few packets of biscuits when he shops, which disappear over a few days. And when they go out with friends, the kids happily order fried food and sugary drinks. Overall, though, it has been relatively easy to eat less processed food simply by removing it from sight. As they don't have so many snacks to fill up on, the kids start eating more of the food I've cooked.

On my part, I wax lyrical about the Ikarians and how they have already helped us make some positive changes, even though I have yet to meet a single islander. I talk to the kids about Ikaria, and they listen in the half-hearted way they always do when an adult enthuses about something, only momentarily looking up from their homework or devices. George listens patiently as I tell him yet another fact about why the Ikarian lifestyle works. I'm beginning to sound like a broken record.

—

The following weekend, I'm sitting reading a quiz about life expectancy when Emmanuel comes into the room and looks over my shoulder.

'Why would you want to know how long you're going to live? That just feels wrong,' he says, making me wonder if my twelve-year-old son is wiser than me.

'What this quiz tells you is how long you're *likely* to live given your behaviour right now. It looks like it's based on statistics and studies about what leads to longer life. It might be fun. There's also one that measures how happy you are.'

Emmanuel casts me a look, as if to say Mum has finally *really* lost it, clearly not convinced that doing a quiz that predicts how long you might live is a good idea.

I found the quiz on a US website called the Blue Zones™ while reading about Ikaria, which is one of the five 'Blue Zones' around the world. These are small regions where people live longer than most of us – up to ten years longer on average, with some individuals living well into their nineties and early hundreds. The Blue Zone areas are diverse: Okinawa in Japan, Sardinia in Italy, Costa Rica in Central America and a community of Seventh Day Adventists in Lorma Linda, California. I see images of a 97-year-old heart surgeon who rides his horse on weekends and a 102-year-old grandmother holding her great, great, great granddaughter in her arms. Their stories confirm what I have already learnt from the Ikarians – that simple daily routines likely help them live longer, healthier lives than most of us.

I watch a talk by Dan Beuttner, a dapper middle-aged man who talks compellingly about what the five Blue Zones communities have in common. He says that we can learn from their lifestyle and diet to add years to our lives and prevent chronic disease such as diabetes, cancer and heart disease. He notes there are no magic pills to longevity, no complicated programs or diets, and that only between 10 and 20 per cent of the factors determining how long we will live are based on our genes.

What all five Blue Zones communities share is that the people keep fit by moving naturally and often. They are compelled to exercise without thinking about it, from planting fruit and vegetables to walking to visit neighbours, to ploughing their fields. They also have a strong sense of purpose, and are often able to articulate exactly why they wake up in the morning – be it to tend their farm, look after grandchildren or simply do work that they enjoy. Their routines shed stress, and prayer, friendship circles and movement all help.

Buettner goes on to talk about how people in these communities eat wisely. They consume mostly plant foods, especially beans. Meat makes up only a small part of their diets. They drink alcohol moderately and regularly, with meals and in company. They stop eating before they feel full, eat their smallest meal in the late afternoon or early evening and don't snack before bed.

I look over at the kids and joke that we could really work on not eating so much …

Emmanuel scoffs. He loves eating and in recent months has started raiding the pantry and fridge every hour of the day. I can't get to the shops fast enough to satisfy his growing appetite.

Social connection is important in the Blue Zones. People have a strong sense of belonging and put their loved ones first. They surround themselves with what Buettner calls the 'right tribe'. He cites evidence showing that if we surround ourselves with happy, healthy people, we are more likely to be happy and healthy ourselves. People in Blue Zones are generally members of faith-based communities. Their ageing parents usually live nearby, they commit to a life partner, and invest in their children with time and love.

The list reminds me to ring my mother more often. To consider eating a little less, yet again. Ponder how we can eat more real food that is quick and easy to prepare when pressing work commitments don't allow us to dedicate much time to cooking.

I think about Emmanuel's words – perhaps it's tempting fate to try to work out how long we're going to live. I switch off the laptop. I don't think I'm quite ready to find out what the quiz will tell me.

—

Reading about the Ikarians has prompted me to read more about health issues in the West – so I pore over every magazine and newspaper article about obesity, movement, social connection, stress and relaxation that comes my way. And I realise I've become a statistic.

I'm one of the nearly two-thirds of people in Australia who are overweight or obese.

I'm one of the many Australians who spend most of my day being sedentary.

I am one of ten Australians each year who experience loneliness.

And like countless people in the Western world, I often feel stressed. I'm not always quite sure how to relax, to enjoy what I have right now.

I am reminded that not only are these things bad for your overall health and wellbeing, they can also shorten your life.

I know I should do something about it, but what? In the absence of a Greek island with clean air, plentiful homegrown foods, an orchard and vegetables to tend to, and a tight-knit village community, what should I do? Should I be going paleo? Eating more 'lite' foods? Taking mindfulness and yoga classes? Selling all our family's earthly possessions and moving to an ashram in India?

All that stuff sounds too hard. Too expensive. And ultimately, not doable or sustainable.

Though I've started to make some small changes, I think I might need some help. Professional help.

—

A few weeks later, I catch up with my friend and former colleague Julie and talk to her about my feelings of malaise. I tell her that even though I am privileged and have so many comforts, I often feel tired, strung out and unable to properly enjoy what I have. We talk about how important it is to appreciate the day-to-day things, and to look after ourselves in order to be able to look after others – but it's easier said than done.

Julie and I worked together in various cancer charities. Around the same time several years ago, we both give up our salaried positions to try and find more balance, to do things we felt passionately about – while still paying our bills and mortgages. I've known Julie since I was in my twenties, and value our friendship. When my father and Katerina died, she comforted me with words that made me feel understood and supported. Now she helps once again by offering to put me in touch with a friend of hers who works at an organisation that might have some answers to my health woes.

A few weeks later, I am sitting in the light-filled office of Jerril Rechter, the CEO of VicHealth, a body that focuses on promoting good health and preventing chronic disease. When we meet, Jerril's already had a few early-morning meetings, and apologises that she needs to rush off to catch an afternoon flight to an international conference soon. We have an hour to get to the bottom of the causes of chronic ill health and what can be done about them. Easy.

Jerril is not shy about sharing with me that, as a former ballerina, she used to go on crash diets and smoke menthol cigarettes in a bid to keep her weight down. She tells me that she gave up smoking when she finished dancing and that no amount of tobacco smoking is safe. Her days of crash dieting are behind her as well – she has more of a 'balanced eating' mindset now, which helps to maintain her energy levels during her busy days.

She then talks about obesity as the 'new smoking' in its widespread impact on health, saying, 'We used to walk through clouds of smoke on the street, in our offices. It was pervasive, it was everywhere, and it just became part of the norm. That is what we're going to be experiencing with obesity. We will have this whole community that is unwell and struggling. It's a huge concern.'

Jerril acknowledges that change is difficult, and that our environment doesn't encourage us to move or to eat well. And it doesn't help that we are so busy.

When I ask her what we should be doing to avoid obesity she says, 'Ultimately, it is around encouraging environments to help us eat well and move more. Around eating fresh fruit, vegetables and whole grains, looking at portion sizes and having a balanced diet. It's also important to build some regular physical activity into your day – whether it's walking your kids to school, taking the stairs instead of the lift at work or if you're out and about, or even getting off the bus or tram a stop early and walking the rest. It should be about your lifestyle and what works for your body to help you maintain a healthy life. It's all about moderation.

'For many people, it can be really hard to live a good life that's active, and to eat well. If you think about quitting smoking, there are tools out there that can help you do it, but ultimately it's hard. I've done it. It's really hard. It's the same with eating well and moving more. We all know that it's important to eat well and move more, but it's changing behaviours that's the hard part!'

She notes that many of us sit for many hours a day – and that there's good research to show that this is shortening our life.

What becomes clear to me is that Jerril is passionate about the idea of investing in our health future, likening it to the way we invest in our financial future, a bit like superannuation for our health.

But she adds that being healthy is not just about food and movement. It's also about social connection.

'Without good social connections, we know people have poor health outcomes, without a doubt,' she says. 'You will die earlier if you are not socially connected. Studies have found that loneliness can be as harmful to our health as smoking fifteen cigarettes a day. It's literally a killer.'

'Everyone's waiting for the next magic pill,' she continues, 'but it's really all about living a good life; eating well and being active. I think everybody should be investing in their health. Little changes every single day are going to really help you live that happier, healthier life as you continue on.'

I'm struck by how the Ikarians have been doing the things Jerril has spoken about all along. Not only that, but what she says reminds me that a lot of this stuff is what we did as kids. Maybe the Ikarian villages are closer to home than I thought ...

—

Late that night, my father's sister, Kanella, rings from her home in southern Greece. As always, she asks about George and the kids, about Mum and Dennis. I tell her that we are well, that I saw Mum and Dennis only a few days ago. Mum was gardening when we arrived, tending the wild greens and herbs in her spring garden, a fact that my *Theia* Kanella appreciates. I ask her what she is growing, and she tells me about her large plot filled with autumn vegetables – the last of the summer tomatoes, cucumber, zucchini, and wild greens as well.

I tell her about my newfound interest in Ikaria. She tells me that one of her sons, my cousin Dionysios, was stationed there as a policeman when he was younger. I remember now that my aunt went over there for his wedding.

She goes on to talk about Ikaria as if it's another planet, not an island in the same country she lives in. 'When I visited, I found them to be a strange people. They open their shops in the middle of the night. They just do what they like, they don't care. They are *anestitoi*, apathetic. Don't worry about Ikaria – just come and visit us,' she concludes.

Rather than putting me off, *Theia* Kanella's comments only serve to pique my curiosity further.

My cousin Sakis from Athens happens to be staying with her. She puts him on the line, and I talk to him about my growing interest in the Ikarians too. He tells me he has spent lots of time on the island – attracted by its harsh beauty and its isolation. The superhot natural springs around the island are good for the congenital spinal condition he has. He speaks reverently of the springs' therapeutic qualities, and reflects on the stark contrast between life in Ikaria and the smog and bustle of Athens.

Sakis also asks when we're coming to Greece. I explain how expensive it would be to bring the whole family, how it's not easy to leave my work.

After I hang up I join George and Emmanuel at the table, pulling a bowl of nuts in their shells towards us, and cracking some to share.

Emmanuel picks up an almond in its shell and asks, 'What are these?'

'Almonds.'

'Oh, so that's where they come from.'

George and I both raise our eyebrows at the same time. We have an almond tree in the garden, though admittedly it hasn't yet provided any fruit.

Emmanuel leaves the table and George asks about my family in Greece. I tell him that my aunt's health is worsening – she has a lung disease, chronic pain from rheumatoid arthritis – but her spirits appear strong. She too asked when we're coming to visit again. George shrugs. A family trip to Greece isn't exactly at the top of our agenda.

'Spiri, you've been talking about this for a while now. Maybe you need to get Ikaria out of your system. You could go on your own. You know we will manage.'

I look at my husband, who I've known for nearly twenty years now. It's moments like this I know I'm with the right man.

'That's good of you, darling, but I can't do it. It's too big a sacrifice, and we can't afford it. I think I'm hankering for this because I need to make some changes.'

'Like what changes?' George asks.

'Well, the way we eat. We've started to eat less processed food, and we're eating more food that we cook ourselves. But still, we eat too much – too much bread and pasta, our portions are quite big, we eat out a fair bit. And we need to move more, sit less. That would be a good start.' I look at George expectantly.

'Well, that sounds ... positive,' he replies, though he looks a bit dubious. Thanks to the Ikarians, he's already started getting off a few stops before he gets to work in order to move more. He's happily eating the healthier meals I make. And he is snacking less on sweet treats each night.

'I'm happy to tweak what we do even more – as long as you don't make me give up bread.'

'I wouldn't dream of it.'

Shifting

Since reading more about Ikaria and the other Blue Zones around the world, I can't help but think more about what's important to me. Sitting down one day, I reflect on the many daily lists I make: what to do, what to buy and how to lose weight. I think about how so many of these lists feel trivial, chronicling the minutiae of my waking hours. I daydream about the things that matter most in my life. Putting pen to paper, I write down three words ...

Family. Health. Creativity.

I stare at the three words I've just scribbled. The list is small, but it may well be the most important one I've ever made.

I think about my family, how much they mean to me and how much energy they take. George and I invest a lot daily in the business of keeping the home fires stoked; keeping the house and garden in a semblance of order, paying off the mortgage, making sure our kids are safe and fed and doing what they're supposed to be doing and happy too. In all this, we try and make time for each other. If we're lucky, there's a little something left over for ourselves.

As parents, George and I try to comfort and guide Dolores and Emmanuel through the awkward land of adolescence as they begin to make their way into adulthood. Being a mother is perhaps the hardest, most rewarding and most relentless job I've ever done. After their births, there was no turning back, no taking the responsibility for another human life away. I would throw myself in front of a car for my children if push came to shove. Their need for me is both daunting and comforting.

As I stare at the word 'family' I wonder, not for the first time, what my life would be like if something were to happen to my children or husband: a terrible accident, a serious illness, a mishap that would change the course of their, and our, lives forever. Or what would it be like if something terrible happened to my brother, Dennis, or my mother? I know from my friend Katerina and from Dad that illness and death can strike at unexpected moments. I remember feeling helpless, at a complete loss as to how to help, but also trying to be with them as much as possible, trying to enjoy the limited time we had and appreciating each moment. I want to spend more time with my mother, in particular.

I know I can't control everything that happens to the people I love, but there are some things I can do. I suddenly realise that making a home – a comfortable nest for my family, where we are fed and feel safe and know that we are loved – is very important to me. It's no wonder I expend so much energy on my family, often at the expense of work or time spent on other things I enjoy.

I look at the word 'health', and understand from my wanderings on the internet these last few months that I've been letting my own health lag behind in my bid to make sure that everyone else is okay. What I've read about the Ikarians has reminded me that health is not just about eating well or even moving more. It's about feeling connected, about having a sense of purpose, feeling that your life is meaningful. I think about the malaise I've been feeling, the sense of needing something exciting to happen to lift me from my stupor, something to reignite the mojo I had when I was younger.

Finally, I reflect on the word 'creativity' and wonder what it is doing there. It sounds so indulgent, so pretentious. But for me, I realise, it's important. To be creative means to make words sing and dance on the page. To be able to make something from the odd vegetables in the bottom of the crisper. To have or listen to an inspiring conversation. To me, it's feeling that you have a special place in the world and are interacting meaningfully with those around you. It is about feeling alive, spirited, vital.

I look at the words for a few more moments and realise I've made a purpose list.

Three words to describe what's most important in my life. It feels like a start.

—

With my newfound focus on things that matter to me, I reconnect with my interest in cooking healthy food and start preparing bigger batches on weekends. This means there is more home-cooked food on hand for the weekdays when we are sometimes too busy to cook.

In keeping with this, I've been taking myself off to my local greengrocer on a more regular basis. The greengrocer is a big shed off a suburban highway. It's a little further away than my local supermarket, but worth the trip as it's easier to place more real food in my trolley there, helping me to plan meals around fresh produce.

Today, I eye the wooden pallet just inside the door, which is heaped high with string beans. Their price has been reduced. Another customer is already expertly looking through them. As I step up alongside her, she moves aside, making room for me.

'They seem alright,' I say, quickly looking over them. It can be a bit hit-and-miss when it comes to the produce in the pallets placed strategically at the door of the greengrocer. The owner runs a warehouse-style operation – and sometimes the produce near the door is a little overripe.

'They're not bad,' she says.

We stand side by side, picking quietly. I plan to use them in the next day or so, before they have a chance to lose their lustre. I look for small, tender and unblemished beans, just like my mother taught me. I love the feeling of knowing what I'm doing, the tactile sensation of handling fresh produce.

'How do you cook them?' I ask the woman.

'In a wok, quite quickly,' she replies. 'Just with some peanut oil, garlic and ginger. Then I add a dash of soy sauce at the end.'

'I do something similar, but I use olive oil,' I say. 'And oregano instead of ginger. I find they look a bit washed out. How do you get them to keep their colour? Do you blanche them in water first?'

'No. I don't worry about it. My son sometimes says to me, "Mum, these don't look like they do in the restaurant." I say to him, "Just eat them. In the restaurant, they add lots of sauces that aren't good for you, too many bad oils. The beans go in your stomach. They don't need to look pretty!"'

I laugh, recognising what seems to be a universal desire to get our kids to 'eat their vegetables'. I can't help but admire this mum's no-nonsense attitude.

'In fact,' she says, 'I crush some garlic and keep it in a jar of oil. Makes things quicker when you get home from work. My mother, and her mother, used to cook the beans this way in China, simply, quickly. No bullshit!' She takes a sideways glance at my hair, my face. 'You're younger than me, but when you get a bit older, you get nostalgic. You go back to the things your people before you did.'

I smile. I'm already there. While I sometimes scoffed at the food my mother cooked when I was a child, yearned for the packaged food of television commercials, I've come to realise that the food she offered us was real food. The more traditional food of her native Greece was simple, wholesome, tasty. I realise now that a lot of it was seasonal, locally sourced – much of it right out of our backyard – and a lot of it was vegetarian. Back then I didn't know that words like 'seasonal' and 'vegetarian' even existed. All I knew was that anything that came out of the garden tasted better than the fruit and veggies we bought from the shops. My father taught me to appreciate garden tomatoes and cucumbers, just picked and washed under the garden hose.

I think of the qualities we ascribe to food today, the wholesale angst around what to eat, and especially what not to eat. There was no angst then – just food that fuelled your body and brought people together around the table to talk and argue and enjoy.

I remember fondly the huge trays of tomatoes and peppers stuffed with rice Mum would cook; the tomato and cucumber salads with lashings of olive oil; the stews she made with green beans, tomatoes and zucchinis, flavoured with dried oregano from our garden. The pots were always large and would usually feed us for a few days. Most of our meals were accompanied by bread, a little feta cheese and some olives Mum had prepared and marinaded herself. The best meals were those shared with cousins and family friends, plates balanced on knees as we sat wherever there was a space at someone's house.

If people dropped in on us, it was no trouble for Mum to quickly whip up 'snacks' of *laganes*, which are fried tendrils of bread, or delicious *loukoumathes* – syrupy donuts sprinkled with walnuts. It was unimaginable for our guests to refuse such treats because they were counting calories, ditching gluten or omitting carbs from their diet.

I want to say to this other mum that I often find myself taking the meandering path back to the Land of the Past, even though I don't have as many grey hairs as her. Not for the first time, I lament that my children aren't more adventurous in their tastes when it comes to the traditional foods of my childhood. It's not really their fault though, because I pandered to their whims when they were younger. When they refused *fakes* (brown lentil soup), or *fasolatha* (bean soup), I stopped offering them. I couldn't imagine exposing them to the more exotic staples of my childhood, like sweetmeats cooked in wine, spinach tossed through with black-eyed beans, or lemony fricassee of celery, herbs and pork.

When I finish picking my string beans, I have a half full bag. My neighbour is still going. I turn to her and say, 'I'll try your method. Thank you.'

'You're welcome,' she replies with a smile.

In the next aisle, I pick up a packet of dried chickpeas. When I get home, I'm going to make a trip to the past.

—

The last time I saw chickpeas being cooked from scratch was in my mother's kitchen as a child. She used to prepare them as a simple soup with freshly grated tomatoes, oil and onions. We had the soup during the last week of Lent – the fasting period before Easter. I remember the tomatoes being fleshy, lush – probably the last of the autumn produce. The soup was oddly comforting, filling.

Even though I don't recall ever cooking chickpeas myself, I know exactly what to do. I grab my biggest pot, half fill it with cold water and pour the chickpeas in. I pick off any that float to the top, as well as any discoloured or misshapen ones. I know that you can add baking soda to the water to help them soften more quickly, but a quick glance at Stephanie Alexander's *The Cook's Companion* suggests this isn't necessary, so I just leave them covered overnight.

The next morning, Sunday, I change the water and put the chickpeas on a slow boil while I potter around. They fill the room with an earthy, wholesome smell that takes me back to Mum's kitchen. I skim the froth from the top once they come to the boil. Approximately two hours later, I turn off the heat while they are still firm but not chalky in the middle. I let them sit a little longer and they plump up nicely, and then I drain them into a large colander. Half a kilo of dried chickpeas, a few dollars' worth, has produced more than a kilo and a half of cooked chickpeas. I could have bought them in a can, but this is much more fun, and more economical. When they've cooled, I put most of them into containers and freeze them to add to stews and throw into salads. The Ikarians would be proud. So would my mother. I need to ring her instead of letting the thought flit in and out of my mind.

Inspired by my memories of tomato soup, I then sauté some onions and garlic in olive oil, adding chopped carrots and celery. I cook the vegetables until they've softened, adding a few pinches of cumin, nutmeg, chilli and cinnamon. After pouring a few cups of the passata we made last summer over the top, I add the chickpeas and a glass of water. I leave it to simmer for half an hour, making the house smell like a Middle Eastern restaurant. Then I season with salt and pepper and they are done.

Soon after, the family sits down to the chickpea stew, served with a side of rice. I haven't put anything else on the kid's plates – too many options and I know they won't touch the chickpeas. While our meals are generally accompanied by bread, it is absent today.

'What's this?' Emmanuel says.

'Chickpea stew.'

'I don't like it.'

'You haven't tried it yet.'

'I know I won't like it,' he insists.

'That's all we have today.'

He takes a small tentative bite, then another. His face tells me they are okay. Bearable. He keeps going. I don't say anything.

Dolores also takes a bite. Looks surprised. 'They're nice, Mum. The spice is nice.'

It's a small coup. Beans have finally made a debut at our family table.

—

A few days after eating the chickpea stew, Dolores and I are standing in front of the yoghurt display case at our local supermarket, which spans several metres of the back wall. When did yoghurt start reproducing? I wonder. This is a whole yoghurt-like family, with cousins and great-aunts and even random guests dropping in. There's yoghurt with fruit, yoghurt with muesli, yoghurt with choc chips. Yoghurt harking from countries around the world, yoghurt with milk that has been stripped of fat, yoghurt with exotic cultures that have been fortified with sugars and vitamins. Further along are the yoghurt-wannabes, strange concoctions in fantastically coloured tubes and chocolate-covered tubs, all promising a quick fix to parental lunchbox dilemmas.

I visualise my *yiayia* standing here, overwhelmed by choice. In her day, she made yoghurt from a single ingredient – the organic milk of her own goats, which roamed the fields behind her home. Later, when she was living with my aunt in the bigger town of Kyparissia in southern Greece, they would have had only a couple of options for yoghurt at the local shop. I remember visiting my aunty when a big national chain supermarket came to Kyparissia – amid great family celebration because it would mean a job for my cousin – and the options for yoghurt multiplied again. Enter yoghurts topped with chocolate chips, muesli and garishly coloured lollies. That's progress for you.

'Can I get this one? I had it at Zoe's. It was nice.' The tub Dolores has in her hand is organic vanilla bean yoghurt, expensively priced. She looks at me hopefully, as if to say, 'this doesn't look like junk'. She knows I mostly buy the Greek yoghurt my mother bought when I was a kid, but it's too sour for her taste. I nod and in the trolley it goes. Eating less processed food isn't going to happen overnight.

As we continue walking around the supermarket, I furtively read the ingredients of this new interloper yoghurt. They number twelve, the second of which is sugar. Despite its name, it doesn't even appear to include real vanilla bean, but a vanilla bean 'mix' – including starch, more sugar, and something called vanilla bean macerates. Even though I'm tempted to put it back on the shelf at this stage (What are vanilla bean macerates exactly?), I don't say anything. I'm trying to buy food that doesn't include a list of ingredients as long as my arm. Food that hasn't been prepared in a factory. It sounds so simple, but when faced with the many thousands of products on supermarket shelves screaming to be taken home, I realise it's going to be a process.

At home, I scoop a little yoghurt into two bowls and add a handful of nuts and berries to the side.

'It's nice, Mum – not too sweet,' says Dolores.

'No, it's quite creamy,' I say. For the moment, I'm determined to enjoy sitting with my daughter, eating together and chatting. I feel secure in the knowledge that I'm starting to cook more of the food that my *yiayia* would recognise, and so eating a little vanilla bean macerates – whatever they are – every now and then isn't going to kill us.

Moving

I'm doing a boxing class at the gym for the first time in months, my fist pumping into the black vinyl. Crack. Crack. Crack. The sound is so satisfying. I'd forgotten that when I'm boxing, my body feels strong. My mind feels strong too, all concentrated energy. I am Rocky Balboa in *Rocky*. Or Maggie Fitzgerald in *Million Dollar Baby*. Before she breaks her neck. I think to myself that I must make the time to do this more often.

'I'm not one to advocate violence, but hit that bag as if your life depends on it,' says Helen, our instructor, with a laugh. I smile through my punches. It's hard to imagine Helen hitting anyone. She's just come back from a few months in India on some sort of spiritual retreat. She's also walked the Camino. When I first saw her heading up an indoor cycling class some five years ago, she was all Greek Goddess, her body lithe and well proportioned, her features classical. I peek at her from behind the bag. Time is leaving its mark on her too – her face is less chiselled, her skin sits more loosely, her body has softened and rounded a little. She seems gentler somehow, less driven.

I look around the room, losing focus for a moment. There are several familiar faces here, people who have been coming for years. There are the serial exercisers, who supplement one or two classes a day with running and gym work and leisurely trips out to the Dandenong Hills to climb a thousand steps on a Sunday morning. There are those, like me, who try and come in a few times a week when we're not too busy, trying to keep on top of the incremental weight gain, needing institutionalised help to meet our quota of rigorous exercise. Many of us are 'Mums with jobs': there's the GP who's trying to shed the weight she gained during pregnancy so she can be a good role model to her patients; the overworked politician who spends too many nights eating out; the new mother who is worried about becoming obese like most of the rest of her family. We try to make a little space in our week to look after our bodies. And our heads. If I let exercise lapse, as I've done recently, I become irritable, mildly anxious. It's not an option to give up fitness classes. Then there are the newbies, who enthusiastically buy a gym membership shortly after the New Year, come to a few classes, and are never to be seen again.

I wonder what my *yiayia* would make of this institution full of sweaty people paying good money to punch boxing bags, cycle on stationary bikes, breathe and stretch while lying on fluorescent mats. What she would make of the things we need to buy to keep fit – lycra workout gear that sticks unflatteringly to the bumps on our bodies, the accoutrements for each new fad class, expensive gym memberships and all manner of gadgets to keep our bodies moving. These things didn't even exist in her vocabulary. Did the word 'fit' even exist?

Yiayia walked, collected wood for her fire, fed her animals each day and did the back-breaking work of harvesting olives each year. The idea of her worrying about her heart rate, burning calories or getting a 'good workout' makes me laugh out loud. I think of the elderly Ikarians, who in the past had no choice but to get around their hilly land on foot or, if they were lucky, on donkeys.

But there are no donkeys here. The gymnasium next door, which I can see through the glass, has sleek exercise machines, all lined up. There are several televisions on, and the people walking or running on the treadmills have ear buds in. They stare straight ahead. Several people on the bikes have their phones out. I haven't been in that part of the gym for many months and I suddenly realise why. It bores me. I make a mental note to walk downstairs after class and ditch that part of my gym membership. I can feel *Yiayia* guiding me. *Bravo, Spiridoula.* Save your money.

—

'We should go. It will get too dark if we don't go on a walk soon,' I say to Dolores a few days later. Spring is morphing into summer, but the long evenings of twilight are still a little way off.

She sighs and goes to her room to put her runners on. Her body language says she'd much prefer to lie on her bed and watch one of the many TV series she is following. But once we're on the way, she walks faster than me, ponytail swinging. I try to keep up.

A few weeks ago, I suggested to Dolores that we start walking together of an evening. The Ikarians have made me think about how we can move more – and how to connect more through our daily rituals. A walk together ticks both boxes. After initial resistance from Dolores ('Mum, aren't you taking this Ikarian thing a bit far?!'), I can see that she now enjoys it.

We make our way up the street, heading towards her old primary school, where we do several laps of the bush track, crunching the gravel to a symphony of rainbow lorikeets and kookaburras. The rhythmic sound of our feet, the movement of our bodies and our snippets of conversation serve to relax us. After we've covered the important topics – what pressing assignments Dolores has due, whether she can go out with friends on the weekend, what I'm working on at the moment – we walk in companionable silence.

I keep waiting for Dolores to hit the difficult teenage years, but she is sensible, mature, contained. Every now and then I tease her, tell her she can deviate from the straight and narrow.

'Why would I want to do silly things, just for the sake of it?' she asks.

Why indeed? Despite my teasing, I'm grateful she has a stable group of friends, that she enjoys school, that she still doesn't mind hanging out with me every now and then.

As we walk, I remember a dream many years ago, in the early days of courtship with George. In it, a little girl, a toddler, stood beside me. I felt an overwhelming sense of love for her, a strong bond I would be hard pressed to describe in words. I woke feeling wistful, knowing that the child in my dream was my daughter.

'Should we do another lap?' Dolores says.

'Maybe just one more,' I reply.

———

When we get home, Dolores flops onto her bed. 'Thanks Mum. That was nice.'

I go out to check on Emmanuel in my studio office. He hasn't moved from the computer since we left, making random internet searches. He's got a YouTube video of the Bees Gees clip 'Staying Alive' playing in the background.

'Where did you find that?' I ask.

'I searched 1970s disco hits.'

I laugh as the impossibly white teeth and pants of Barry Gibb flash by, and soon Emmanuel and I are dancing, gyrating around the study, trying to reproduce Travolta's athletic moves. It's near impossible on carpet and Emmanuel manages better than I, although he is impressed with my face waves and disco points.

'Where did you learn to do that, Mum?'

'In front of the mirror. This is the music I grew up to.' I check the date on the clip. 'I was seven years old when this came out,' I huff through knee knocks.

By the time the clip finishes, we've worked up a decent sweat and the step counter the family got me for Christmas has buzzed. Even though I haven't done any formal exercise today, I've reached my 10,000 steps. We walk back to the house through the garden, and Emmanuel wants to lie on the grass like he did as a kid. He invites me to join him. The first stars have just come out.

'If you could solve the problem of world hunger, but I had to die, would you choose to save me, or get rid of hunger?' he asks as we're lying there.

'Emmanuel, you know I can't answer that.'

'You *should* choose to end world hunger.'

'I know that in my head. But in my heart, I would want to save you.'

Emmanuel asks more thorny questions that I can't solve, until I finally drag myself up. 'These dilemmas are going to have to wait for the morning. I can't keep up.'

—

Later, I join George in bed. Thinking of a young Travolta in shiny spandex shirt, impossibly tight pants, chunky platform heels, I let out a guffaw.

'What's so funny?' George asks.

'I wonder how John Travolta would go dancing to "Staying Alive" now,' I reply, thinking of the recent photos I've seen of him, and how he looks considerably stouter than he did in his heyday. Then again, so do I.

George rolls his eyes. He simply can't understand the thing I have for disco music and cheesy dance movies.

He goes back to his book and I switch off my bedside light, happily tired, 'Staying Alive' playing on repeat in my head.

Lazing

It's now the summer holidays and I'm enjoying having more time with the kids, visiting family more often, reading more books. Mum is pleased – we have visited her a few times in the past few weeks. She has picked cucumbers and tomatoes from her garden, cooked massive amounts of home-cut chips for the kids. While the kids recover from the excesses on the coach, I rejoice in the time I have with Mum to catch up on news and gossip a little.

Time seems to slow now that we don't have to get up early for school runs. The Ikarians are never far from my mind, and I reflect that they seem to intuitively follow the rhythms of the day, rather than forcing time to submit to their whims. While the dream of going to Ikaria is still in the back of my mind, I'm more aware that there is a lot to enjoy right here in our own home – the washing blowing in the early morning sun, the hammock swinging under the olive tree, our cat stretching out over the curve of the wood-fired oven.

With a bit more time on our hands, I wake early to work. Then George and I potter around our home, doing projects that have lapsed during the year – clearing the garage, washing windows, decluttering cupboards.

When George returns to work, meal times become lax, the meals even more improvised that usual. Today, we're having a tub of leftover ragout mixed in with some ripe tomatoes to make it go further, and spooned over pasta. I call the kids and we take lunch out to a small garden table in the shade. Dolores brings water and glasses. Emmanuel pulls in a third seat from the garden. When Dolores gets up to get some more glasses, Emmanuel claims her more comfortable seat. They bicker. Automatically, I consider trying to bring the argument to a close, but it blows over quickly and soon we are eating the pasta ragout.

'It's good Mum,' says Emmanuel. For him, having only woken an hour before, this is breakfast. 'Is there any more?'

There is, and he gets himself another bowl. The ragout is better than it was a few days ago when George made it: the flavours have settled; the sauce is thicker. I see Dolores eyeing Emmanuel's plate enviously. She too wants seconds, but is resisting the urge.

After we eat, Emmanuel lies face down on the deck, in the same way he did as a young child, only now he is much longer, his body more angular.

'You look like a lizard in the sun,' I say.

He smiles, stretching his legs and putting his cheek to the warm boards that line this part of the garden.

'Can I pour water over you?' asks Dolores, holding the dregs of her glass up to her brother, grinning.

'Okay.'

As she pours the water down his back, Emmanuel wriggles and laughs at the shock of the cold liquid on his warm back. It seeps into the fabric of his pyjama top.

There are peach pits strewn at my feet. The possums have had their fill of the fruit before us. Getting up, I find three peaches from our tree that are almost ripe. I wash them and give one to each of my kids. Mine has some insects and a tiny worm in it, and I carefully cut around these and throw them into the garden, just as my mother did when I was a child. The kids look on, intrigued. I'm not letting the peach go to waste. While it's a little too firm, and not quite sweet enough, the flavour trumps anything I have bought from the shops recently.

Emmanuel gives Dolores permission to pour another glass of water over him. She then takes the jug and holds it up expectantly. Emmanuel nods. I am surprised at the burgeoning relationship that is subtly unfolding between our children – nuanced looks that signal agreement, spontaneous hugs, laughter at shared jokes – which was unimaginable a few years ago.

Emmanuel squirms and giggles as Dolores pours the water on his back, down his legs, into the neck of his t-shirt. Soon he is lying in a small puddle of water. I watch as the sun dries its edges out. We talk, comfortably full and in no rush to move.

The dishes are piled up beside us. I am aware that there are chores that await inside, as always – the washing that needs to be brought in, the emails that need to be sent, the floor that could do with a vacuum. And as I do them, the kids will probably wind their way back to their devices, talking to their friends or playing games. This is a small moment of grace in our day. I'm determined to savour it for as long as possible.

—

There's no turning back from the knowledge that my sedentary lifestyle was literally robbing me of years of life. I've become very conscious in recent months of how I can move about in my own 'village' more. I need the change to be easy for me – otherwise I won't keep it up. And I don't want it to take up too much time. And so, when I'm out, I've started walking up escalators, taking stairs rather than lifts, standing rather than sitting when on the train, and parking my car a little further at shopping centres rather than aiming for the spot closest to the entrance. None of this takes me any extra time, but it means that I move more.

I feel more energetic, feel nicely tired at the end of the day. I sleep better and wake up with more energy. And in coming days I'm going to need the energy – we've been putting off a big household chore, but there's no holding off any longer. We need to move our son into a bigger room.

Emmanuel's bedroom is like a well-organised op shop: boxes of soft toys and Lego atop the wardrobe; model planes, cars, snow domes and other miscellanea on the bookshelf; collections of radios that have been pulled apart, paddle pop sticks that have yet to be put together, football cards and magnets and dried-out textas in drawers; a bucket of old garage hinges from a metal detecting trip in a dusty corner ... It's amazing what a boy collects over the course of his childhood. Particularly a boy who finds it hard to part with stuff.

Despite our best efforts to trim and cull over the years, Emmanuel has now outgrown his small room. After a sudden growth spurt, his legs hang over his bunk bed and his head hits the ceiling every time he gets up. We've decided to move him across the hall to the lounge room. Having prepared for a few weeks now, the stage is set – a bigger bed and a new desk are waiting to be set up. An office chair stands in the hallway. We're ready.

We earmark a day when everyone is home for the 'exchange'. I brace myself to beg and plead that some of Emmanuel's stuff goes to the op shop, or to a new home with a little boy who will enjoy Emmanual's things as much as he did. I'm not so worried about the marathon of cleaning and culling, scrubbing and creating. In fact, I'm looking forward to it.

The process starts early in the morning. We decide to empty the room first, and I start carting box after box, pile after pile to the study in the back garden. We dismantle the bed. Take out the rest of the furniture. Vacuum and dust and scrub the walls. Remove the furniture from the lounge and try and squeeze some of it into

Emmanuel's old room. Put the bed and new desk together. And slowly start to put some of his stuff back in the new room.

Normally I would grumble my way through such a project – but I'm pleased to be able to help Emmanuel organise a new teenage room that he can move about in and put his own adolescent stamp on. My fitness tracker vibrates at midday – I've hit 10,000 steps already and we haven't even made a dent. It feels good to exercise without thinking about it.

As I'm trying to scrub texta marks and odd bits of tape off the walls, I think how the Ikarians and other Blue Zoners keep active throughout the course of their days without going to the gyms, lifting weights or standing on a vibrating machine. The thought is liberating.

—

That night, we admire Emmanuel's new room. He has a clean new desk, a bookshelf that isn't crammed to the gills, and a new bed that he fits into. It's taken a fair bit of work, but we got there. We're both tired and pleased.

By the time I have a shower and get into bed, I've clocked up 22,000 steps – and I haven't left our home once today.

Socialising

Fiona and I part to avoid a cyclist, our runners crunching the gravel and bright autumn leaves underfoot. Around us there are dogs on leashes, toddlers in prams, primary-school-aged children rubbing sleep from their eyes as their parents cajole them into keeping up on their way to school. While I enjoyed the ritual of taking the kids to school when they were younger, I'm relieved that part of my life is behind me.

We are on what has become one of our regular Friday morning walks now that the weather is cooling again, which starts 'first thing' at 8.30 after we've packed our teenagers off to school, put a few loads of washing on, made sure our beds are done and so on. One of us is usually late having tried to fit in as many domestic chores as possible. But we both look forward to our walk and rarely cancel.

We walk along the bush track that starts at the primary school our children attended. The kids are at different schools now and only see each other every now and then. For Fiona and I, though, what started as an occasional stroll and coffee after we'd dropped the kids off has morphed into a regular brisk walk and a gabfest before our family-focused weekends.

Invariably, the talk turns to our children. We often share our small frustrations as we bumble our way through parenting in the age of devices. It's us against the seductive flash of the iPhone and the sexy bleep of the Xbox, the Siren-like calls which seem to lure our children away from us. The devices are 'Responsible for All Our Problems'. They stop our children from talking to us. From doing their homework or reading a book. From getting out and being active. Why can't they just put them away?!

But we both know we're just venting, and that we are lucky. Our kids are healthy and still look to us for opinions and advice. They tell us the things that concern them. They still want to come out with us. They don't take drugs, aren't experimenting with alcohol – at least not yet. And they haven't fallen in with a 'bad crowd'.

I hear echoes of my parents in my own voice. When I was a young woman, my father used to warn me against falling in with *kakies parees* – bad company – saying that rot quickly spreads. I remember my teenage self – eager to have more edgy experiences, to grow up quickly and do things I knew Dad wouldn't approve of. I don't see that same pressing drive in my own children. At least I *hope* my son is just joking when he says he wants to fight drug cartels on the streets of Rio di Janeiro as soon as he is old enough to leave home.

I think back to the friendships I had as a young person. I was always drawn to strong women who spoke their minds and lived their lives passionately – we made mistakes together, picked each other up after failed relationships, ate and drank and danced our way well into the small hours of the morning. Some of these friendships have burned themselves out, but some are still going, albeit constrained by the commitments of our respective lives. I continue to catch up with my friend Stacey, who I've known for more than twenty years. I smile at how pressing our existential angst seemed when we were younger, when we would snuggle into the couch of her inner-city apartment, talking non-stop and smoking; how feverishly our hips swayed as we danced on tables at beachside bars on Greek islands, walking home in stilettos as the sun came up.

Now, we both have teenagers and husbands, mortgages and ageing parents. Our six-monthly catch-ups are often qualified with, 'I'm working early tomorrow, so I can't stay out too late ...'

The last time we met, Stacey ordered chamomile tea and I stopped at one glass of wine. We complained that the music was too loud to hear each other talk. Stacey was worried about her eldest child going to schoolies, proudly showing me photos of a well-dressed young man smiling at the camera on his way to the school formal. She told me she was trying to keep body and soul together by doing yoga, practising mindfulness. We tittered at some of the more cultish forms of yoga she'd tried over the years. One, involving the signing of a confidentiality clause and animalistic grunts under the cover of darkness, had us snorting in laughter. She talked about how she'd joined an outdoor fitness class, which was the only thing that had worked so far in allaying her menopausal symptoms. I said how boxing was one of the few acceptable ways I could vent anger. Three hours flew past without us noticing as we careened between the nostalgia-tinged past and what was concerning us now.

Fiona and I have wound around the track, past the shops and back to the car park, where we will take up our day again. She needs to shop for food and pick up one of her kids for a medical appointment later in the afternoon; I need to finish a report I'm working on.

'What are you having for dinner tonight?' I ask Fiona, who is a fine cook.

'I'm just going to cook a quick pasta with a pesto of peas, basil, mint, garlic and oil,' she replies. 'I need to get my boys to basketball, and it only takes 15 minutes.'

Like me, Fiona enjoys cooking. When she has time, she plans delicious meals based on seasonal ingredients. I respect her culinary opinion, and often feel inspired to head straight to the shops after our walks to pick up an ingredient that I've forgotten about or haven't thought to use before. Once again, I'm inspired to try this new recipe. It sounds easy – and something my kids are likely to eat.

Before long, our cars come into view and we hug.

'Take care. See you next week …'

'I look forward to it.' And I do.

—

Over the years, I've avoided socialising during work hours in a bid to get work done – but since meeting the Ikarians, I realise that socialising and getting work done need not be mutually exclusive. I need to get out of my office more, and feed my desire to talk with and connect with people. In keeping with this, today I'm having lunch with my friend Nic, a writer and teacher. We are in the café at the Heide Museum of Modern Art, dappled autumn sunshine filtering through the large windows. The museum is on the grounds of the former home of art benefactors John and Sunday Reed. Now it's made up of a kitchen garden, a café and gallery, as well as the original homestead.

George and I used to bring Dolores and Emmanuel here when they were little. They would run around the metal sculptures dotting the grounds, touch and smell the herbs in the garden, and marvel at the extravagant cat-run attached to the homestead.

I think sadly about how the last time we were here as a family was with my friend Katerina. We had bought her an overpriced lunch box that she didn't touch. 'Could this be it, Spiri?' she had asked me when the kids were away from earshot. A week later, she had passed away.

It's mid-week and the café is full. After spending so much time at home, it feels strange that so many people are out in the middle of the day, enjoying themselves. Lunching. Drinking. Laughing. I order a glass of wine so that I too might be part of the festive throng.

'You should consider teaching, Spiri,' says Nic. 'You'd be a natural. And we're in need of more staff where I work.'

It's not the first time Nic has suggested such an idea. But in the past I've always been too busy trying to run my fledgling business and raise our young family. Getting my certificate to teach in tertiary education felt too hard. It was yet another bit of paper I didn't have the time or extra cash to get. Now, though, the sociable Ikarians have got me thinking that I need to get out more, see more people each day. Perhaps this is the answer?

I met Nic when I did a corporate writing unit in a professional writing course. I'd won a prize for a story about Dad's village. I'd written it while our family were staying with my aunt Kanella in southern Greece. The story slipped out of me after we'd visited Dad's family home. I'd put the kids to bed, then stayed up well after midnight, my fingers flying across my cousin's laptop keyboard, barely able to keep up with my racing thoughts, eager to capture the emotional vein of the story. As soon as it was down, it felt as if I'd written something special. I'd quickly funnelled the prize money back into paying for a corporate writing unit to help with my business before I could spend it on bills and food shopping.

Nic has since encouraged and supported my writing, and every now and then we catch up for lunch and debrief about the trials and tribulations of running businesses out of a home office. He seems to have a lot more work on than me, seems to be able to get out of his office more. I find myself feeling a little envious as Nic reels off the many projects he is working on – teaching, writing books, taking his kids to basketball, thinking about a movie script.

I am in awe of his energy. But I can't help it. My mothering instinct kicks in, perhaps to avoid thinking about the changes I might need to make to my own life.

'Take it easy, Nic. You need to have breaks. When was the last time you had a day off?'

Nic laughs. 'Maybe several years ago. I can't remember.'

'Promise me you'll take a day off soon. Put it in the diary. You need to schedule it in.'

'What about the teaching then?' he counters. 'Just do the training course. Send me your CV. I'll pass it on to my manager.'

I think about my lonely office, wonder if getting out a few days a week would do me good. I reflect that the Ikarians would never sit in a room all day, tapping at a computer, not talking to anyone. I find myself getting excited about imparting knowledge about my craft. About honouring it even more.

As we part, Nic agrees to schedule in a day off and I promise to have a think about teaching. The seed that he's sown is starting to germinate.

—

Inspired further by the social Ikarians, I'd put a call out to start a book club. I'd been part of a book club years ago, where we argued about Christos Tsiolkas's *The Slap* or waxed lyrical about Marilynne Robinson's *Gilead*. But we were all busy people who lived in different suburbs, and in the end the logistics of coordinating dates and venues beat us.

I learnt from this lesson, and so opted to ask only local people. I wanted to make it easy for them to come out of their homes mid-week. I would provide the venue; all they had to do was read the book and bring food or wine to share. Most of the women I invited were mums I'd spent time talking to at the school line-up. Dolores is still good friends with their children. I didn't expect one of the perks of the group to be the exchange of information and a light-hearted debriefing on the challenges of parenting teenagers. A free therapy group over gooey cheese, prosecco and literature.

Our group meets again, and we walk through our early winter garden towards the study where the lights and heater are on. George has got some soft jazz playing. I have set out wine glasses, and each member places something to share on the table – soft cheese and crackers, chocolate, biscuits, fruit. We pass around the cheese, pour wine, sit back.

The Ikarians have prompted me to think about eating less, but it's challenging to put into practice when faced with foods I love – tonight, I keep going back to the cheese, chipping away at it, even after my fellow book clubbers have slowed down.

In a bid to eat less, I'm trying to take a gradual and non-punitive approach: putting slightly smaller portions on my plate, replacing sweet treats with nuts and seeds from the pantry, and eating smaller serves of bread and pasta, making up for it with larger serves of salads and vegetables. I'm more conscious of avoiding late night snacking, taking myself off to bed rather than raiding the pantry for my nightly energy boost. And I've been trying to listen to my hunger cues, eating when I'm hungry rather than when I'm bored or a bit flat. It's all helped – I've sliced a few inches off my waistline over several months without even trying. But faced with the seductive lure of soft cheese, or potato chips, or salty crackers, my resolve leaves me.

Tonight, we're discussing Viet Than Nguyen's *The Sympathizer*, but as usual the conversation has strayed to our children – how they're going at school, how we can pull them away from the seductive lure of their devices, who they might be kissing. We don't really *know* who they're kissing, if they're kissing anyone at all, but part of the joy is wondering and scheming how we can find out. As we drink more wine, the conversation gets bawdier. We're a bunch of middle-aged mums, but something younger and freer comes out. We let loose in the safe confines of our messy study – then we can each go back to our families more responsible, more contained. More mature.

While it's not stated, each of us bring the things we like the most. Jill always brings cheese. Leah always sweets. Georgia wine. Invariably, I scrounge in the fridge or pantry a little before book club, wondering what my contribution will be. I'm determined that this group is not going to be yet another stress, but a joyful gathering to talk about books.

I finish the cheese and take a sip of prosecco,.

And while I know that I'll regret it tomorrow as I move sluggishly through the day, tonight I enjoy this little feast.

Reflecting

'Mighty Greek warrior in the siege of Troy. First letter "A".'

'Adam?'

It's late in the evening and the requisite ancient heroes, whose names were drummed into me at Greek school, will simply not reveal themselves to me. 'Adam' might be right – but he doesn't sound mighty enough. Biblical yes, mighty no.

George and I are lying in bed, the paper between us. We started the crossword a little after six this morning. George is more alert than me in the mornings and usually wakes up in a sociable mood. Irritatingly, he wakes at the same time on weekends. It was a running joke between us early in our marriage that the only reason I would ever leave him is because he gets up so early. After seventeen years of the same, I'm *almost* used to it. I would never admit it to him, but I even appreciate having the quiet hours of the morning before the kids wake so I can potter, or read, or get some pressing work done before the day starts properly. And it would be ungracious of me to complain too much – he generally delivers coffee to my bedside.

Still, I need at least half a cup of coffee before my brain can do the required linguistic gymnastics to get through the crossword. This morning we managed to get halfway through it before the kids shuffled into the kitchen, sleepy eyed and monosyllabic. We gave them some clues over breakfast, and they were pleased to get a couple of answers in.

The day continued, and the paper sat on the kitchen table. Over lunch, I glanced at it again. I got a few more answers, snapped a pic of it with my phone and sent it to George at work. From the train home, he sent me three texts with answers – we're nearly there. Just a few more and we're done. It's not often that we get all the way to the end.

Years ago, George would tease me for occasionally doing the crossword in the Saturday papers. Didn't I have anything better to do? But now that we're older, there's a tacit understanding that we need to keep our brains active, and the crossword is one of those rituals that helps us connect in a way which doesn't involve discussions about who's taking the kids where, what bills need to be paid or how we're going to manage to squeeze in seeing our parents on the weekend.

When George and I first got married, George's mother, Dolores, said that to have a successful relationship you each need to be patient. His father, Alfred, said, 'In a relationship, the bread must be baked fresh daily.' I think of that every time George and I let our relationship lapse in small ways – when I realise we haven't spoken all day, or I've been remiss in communicating something important, or I'm holding in some little resentment. It's then, to use the corny analogy, I think about stoking the fire, kneading the bread, sliding it into the oven, and making a fresh loaf.

The things we do aren't profound, extravagant gestures. We don't often go on formal dates. We rarely go away together. We don't deliver impromptu bunches of flowers. But we still manage to flirt at the accountant's office while we do our annual tax, casting smouldering glances while the agent taps his numbers in, playing footsies under the table. We walk hand in hand in furniture stores on our 'suburban dates', trying to solve our storage issues. And when we work together on blog assignments where I am the Writer and he is the Photographer, we pretend not to know each other, giving each other sly kisses when our client isn't looking.

My father-in-law didn't divulge how we might keep the feeling of *wanting* to bake the bread daily – he just said that's what we needed to do. I'm grateful that we still both want to put the work in. And that we still want to play.

A few years back, when George started watching *The Sopranos*, I sat through the first episode with him, but I couldn't get my head around the thick New Jersey Italian accents. And I thought it might be a better use of my time to read rather than commit to dozens of episodes of violent mafia action. Every few nights, I'd hear George guffawing, or calling out to the television as shots were fired and profanities slipped under the loungeroom door. When he came to bed, he would explain to me who Tony had slept with, how Uncle Junior was undermined yet again, or described the latest family dynamics in vivid and juicy detail.

'How can you laugh at all that violence?' I would ask, perplexed and not a little disturbed. How well did I *really* know my husband?

George had explained that the violence was part of the beauty of the series. He talked about the way you sympathise with the main character, even if you don't agree with his actions; the way he drew you in with the seductive pull of his power, even when you knew what he was doing was morally wrong. Despite myself, I began wishing I'd persevered with the show so I could contribute more meaningfully to the conversation. I vowed that we would watch whatever the next series George got interested in together.

Last year, when the final thrilling episode of *The Sopranos* was over, we agreed to watch *Mad Men*, with most Friday nights allocated to the job. I would prepare gin and tonics in cocktail glasses, the rims encrusted with sugar and lemon juice. George would cut up a few pieces of dark chocolate, prepare a little bowl of almonds. And with our preparations ready, we would immerse ourselves in the world of 1960s advertising: breasts held high in Playtex bras, silk stockings clipped on with suspenders; elegant male frames clad in crisp white shirts, sharp suits and ironed boxers. The exquisite wardrobes hiding characters who were deeply flawed and unhappy, their dissatisfactions juxtaposed against the slick commercialism of the advertising world. While the episodes invariably left us feeling a little flat, they always led to interesting discussions. George was often left hankering for the antics of Tony Soprano – at least he was passionate in his emotions: fiery, loyal, fierce – even if he was a serial womaniser and murderer. The characters in *Mad Men* didn't even seem to *like* each other.

Back in bed that night, I resign myself to not completing the crossword. 'I don't think it's Adam. That doesn't ring a bell.' I give George a kiss, and turn to switch off the light.

The next day, we meet around the table again at 6.30, a fresh paper in front of us.

George turns to the crossword answers. I turn to my coffee, bleary eyed.

'Ajax.'

'Of course. I knew that.'

—

As I peel vegetables for our dinner, I reflect that it has been around a year since I 'met' Stamatis and other Ikarians via the internet. And while the fantasy of visiting the island is still alive in my mind (I will go there *one day*), the Ikarians have already inspired me to make many changes.

As a family, we are eating more foods that my *Yiayia* would have recognised – legumes, beans, wholegrains and vegetables. We've also started eating more seasonally – cabbages in winter;

asparagus in spring; eggplant, tomatoes and basil in summer; pumpkins in autumn. The kids have had lots of culinary firsts – from that initial taste of chickpea stew, to eating freshly cut coleslaw with a splash of olive oil and vinegar the way my mother used to make it, to trying walnuts straight from their shells. Each week I've tried to offer a serve of beans and a serve of fish to replace our default of meals mased on red meat and chicken. I'm using more herbs and spices to flavour our food, largely avoiding pre-packaged sauces and stocks. While the kids are not always enthusiastic, most of the time they don't even notice.

I find we are moving a lot more as a family. As well as my 'walks and talks' with Dolores, the two of us have been going to dance exercise classes together now that the weather is cold. Emmanuel has set an alarm on his phone to remind him to move at regular intervals. George is still getting off a few stops away from his work to fit in a walk. I now understand that despite my love-hate relationship with housework (why can't it just stay *done*?), it keeps me moving and helps me feel like I can impose some sort of order on the chaos that is family life. If there are clean socks, the kitchen bench is crumb-free and the toilet clean, it feels as if *everything will somehow work out*. I have to continually remind myself that while the work is unpaid, it is valuable.

Once again, the winter fills me with a vague sense of longing to be elsewhere, and I find I am at a crossroads yet again – should I invest in going to Ikaria or in changing my life here? After some deliberation and discussion with George ('Are you *still* thinking about Ikaria?' A little less patient now), changing my life here wins out. Though visiting a sunny Mediterranean island is seductive, it's a temporary fix to my ills. I need a longer-term solution. And so, I decide to heed Nic's advice and find a job that will get me out of the house more. I consider taking the required training to teach writing, and find a fast-tracked course that isn't prohibitively priced. I take the course, go for an interview where Nic works, and soon I have a job teaching writing at a university not far from our home. I reflect that once again I have transformed myself – from social worker at the start of my career, to writer, to teacher. I look forward to starting next month.

I've become more aware of prioritising my most important relationships. I am conscious that Dolores and Emmanuel are growing up fast; I need to spend time with them while I can, despite the challenges of balancing work and other responsibilities. And George and I need to keep looking after each other, connecting in small ways each day.

Every now and then, the kids tease me about my 'Ikarian phase', rolling their eyes when I offer yet another new vegetable to try, or when I prise them from their devices to go for a walk or do some spontaneous daggy dancing. But I think the lessons I've learnt from the Ikarians have moved beyond a phase. They are here to stay.

My gut is moving better and I'm rarely going to bed with indigestion these days. My energy levels are more balanced, with fewer big energy slumps during each day. I try to get to bed at a reasonable hour when I am tired, rather than eating to give me one more energy kick. And I'm feeling more optimistic, more connected to myself and those around me.

I wonder, not for the first time, if the changes I have made might affect how long I am likely to live. After I pile the vegetables into a colander, on a whim, I fire up my laptop and search for 'Blue Zones longevity test'. The idea of finding out about my life expectancy no longer fills me with fear. I have much better control over my health than I did a year ago. And better control over my thinking.

The Blue Zones website flashes up and all it takes is a few minutes to answer questions about my lifestyle habits. Things like my gender, how many serves of fruit and vegetables I eat, how much exercise I do. The test reports that, given my current lifestyle habits and profile, I have a life expectancy of ninety-three. The figure is surprising and pleasing, especially as the report says that many of those years could be spent free of chronic illnesses such as heart disease and diabetes. It goes on to suggest I could do a range of things to increase the number of years I live, including eating more whole fruit, eating less salt and building in relaxation rituals.

I do the corresponding test that measures my happiness rating. When I see the result, I feel like a kid who has topped the class. A+.

If the truth be told, I'm not surprised. I am the happiest and healthiest I've been in a very long time.

Fearing

The landline trills several times, stops, then goes again. I'm just about to finish a work call on my mobile. I cut it short and pick up the home phone. 'Mum's not making sense, she put a knife in her mouth,' says my brother, who sounds on the edge of panic. 'Oh my god, I don't know what to do, what should I do?'

I try to slow him down, work out what's happened, find out where Mum is now, whether she is safe, but he isn't making sense. It's as if he's suddenly gone from being a middle-aged man to a boy.

'I'll be right there. Call an ambulance,' I say, feigning calm.

After I hang up I don't trust myself to get up for a moment. My knees are weak. I know something is terribly wrong.

I lurch into my car and speed towards my mother's home, arriving to find two neighbours at the door and an ambulance outside. In the kitchen, my mother is sitting in a chair, looking distressed and babbling indecipherably.

My brother looks wild-eyed. Mum was cooking, he tells me, when she started choking and tried to remove what was in her mouth with a knife.

At the hospital, the doctors do test after test in quick succession and then tell me she has had a stroke. A doctor shows me on a scan that the communication part of her brain has been deprived of blood and oxygen. It is severely damaged. It's also what caused the choking reflex. They will administer a clot-busting drug.

My aunt, cousin and niece somehow appear in front of me and I greet them in the chaos of the emergency room, dazed and distracted by doctors and bleeping machines. They leave after a time, and I pace, wait, hold Mum's hand helplessly, the windowless rooms adding to my sense of unreality. George rings wanting to know if he and the kids should come in. I tell him I don't want the kids to see *Yiayia* like this. Maybe tomorrow.

Several hours later, it appears the drug has stopped the stroke from causing any more harm. As Mum is monitored in intensive care, she falls in and out of sleep. When she wakes, I struggle to understand what she is saying. She speaks in monosyllables, the words she wants to say coming out all wrong. Young resident doctors come in and use words like dysphasia and dyspraxia. They can't be sure how the impact of the stroke will play out, how much function she will get back, only time will tell.

I still can't believe this is happening to my mother, who has always been so healthy and lively. I reply in the negative to every question the doctors ask. No, she didn't have high cholesterol or high blood pressure. No heart problems. She wasn't on any medications. She barely visited doctors. What I forget to tell them is that the day before yesterday was the eleventh anniversary of Dad's death – we had gone to church to commemorate it, and she was upset that he was no longer with us. I don't tell them that she worries about everyone. That she still travels at a pace that would put a fifteen-year-old to shame.

Across from Mum's bed is a man who has had a stroke worse than hers. His family gathers around him at all hours. When Mum wakes, she realises they are speaking Greek. She tries to ask me what is wrong with the man, and I explain that he's had a very serious stroke.

'*O kakomiris*. The poor man.' It's the first clear thing she has said.

The next morning when I come in, the man's wife is sitting beside Mum. The doctors have told her that her husband won't make it. Despite her own bad news, the woman is comforting Mum, telling her that things will be alright, that it could have been worse, that at least she is alive. Mum is trying to say how hard it is for her, how she has lost her words, that she can't speak properly. She looks lost and confused.

I sit down, trying not to disturb them. They embrace tightly, and cry into each other's shoulders. I hear Mum say clearly, '*Yerasame stin Australia.* (We've grown old in Australia.)' I sob, a silent witness between two strangers who share only their language and a primal desire to help the other.

Later that day, the man is taken to a private room to die with his family and friends around him. Mum gets out of bed for the first time and conveys to me with hand gestures and garbled words that she wants me to help her find the room so that she can see how the family is.

I know then that I haven't lost my mother – her amazing capacity to empathise and connect is still there. Her spirit is strong. All this time I have been looking across the seas to the Ikarians – but the most resilient and spirited person I know has been with me all along.

Family and friends who have come to visit Mum spill out of the hospital room. A family friend who is a nurse tries to explain in simple Greek to Mum that her brain's language centres have been damaged by the stroke. My godparents are here too, always at the ready when there is a family crisis. Cousins and aunties and uncles congregate outside the door, taking it in turns to come in and see Mum. The nurses have explained that Mum will be overwhelmed, won't be able to take too much in at any one time, will tire easily. While I realise that this is the case, I also see that having people around her who love her is good for Mum's spirits, as it is for mine.

—

Hours turn into days and I fall into a routine of sorts. In the mornings I go into the hospital early in a bid to catch the doctors. I become Mum's voice, ask the questions I think she'd want to ask but can't. In those first scary days in intensive care, I had skirted around the thought that preoccupied us all: would she pull through?

Now she's on the ward, I want to know if there is a chance she is likely to have another stroke, how much capacity she will get back. The doctors poke and question and order test after test, but in the end, they have few sureties to offer. Mum looks on, blinking helplessly. Later, she asks with difficulty, 'What did they say? Will I get better?' While I don't understand all her words, I understand the feeling behind them, sense her fear. I focus on the positives. She might be able to make major improvements, but it will take work. She needs to take it one day at a time. She is not alone, we will support her. *Why me? Why me?* she laments over and over.

Once I've spoken to the doctors and before any visitors arrive, my phone pings constantly with friends and family wanting to know how Mum is, if there is anything they can do to help, whether it's okay to visit. The messages are comforting, making me feel as if the village has stepped up, surrounding us. It attests to Mum's generosity over the years. Now that she needs people, they are here for her too.

While Mum sleeps during the day, I have time to think. I reflect on how suddenly things in life can change – there I was, worried about my life not being exciting enough. I'm now worried about what life would be like without my mother. The thought is sobering. It makes me think about how much she means to me and appreciate her even more. I vow to do my best not to get frustrated when she offers me one too many zucchini fritters. To ring each day, even if it's only for a few moments. And to visit more.

After spending whole days at the hospital, I get home late at night. George has the garage light on as I pull in and warms food as soon as I step in the door. I am stiff from sitting for so long in a hospital chair, and my hands smell of hospital disinfectant. Our house is cosy, and George's embrace and the banter of the children as they tell me about their day is comforting. It makes me appreciate anew what I have here, how warm it is.

—

Within a week of Mum's hospitalisation, her medical team have formed a plan. Mum's blood pressure and cholesterol, two crucial risk factors for stroke, are stable. While she now has a higher risk of having another stroke – by virtue of the fact that she has had one already – the doctors and nurses have done the best they can do to prevent it happening again. We are going to move Mum to a rehabilitation facility, where she will have a bevy of treatments. She wants to know when she will be ready to return home. They can't say.

I go back and forth to the family home to bring back things she needs: clean nighties, underclothes, slippers, food that family and friends have brought over during their visits. For many days immediately after the stroke, Mum had been trying to tell me, my brother, and my cousins something pressing, but couldn't find the words. Eventually, we gathered that she wanted us to harvest the broccoli in her garden and share it around. At her house, I fill three large supermarket bags of broccoli, my feet sinking into the wet earth of her garden. When I arrive at the hospital that day and tell her the task is done, she looks immensely relieved. Now the harvest won't go to waste.

We move Mum to a rehabilitation hospital on a hill near her home. It feels familiar and safe; we have driven past it hundreds of times. Its large windows overlook bushland. After we place her things in a light-filled room, I introduce myself and Mum to a middle-aged woman who will be sharing the room. I learn the woman fell down the stairs of her two-storey house, and is recovering from a head injury.

In the days and weeks that follow, I meet many others like this woman, people whose lives have taken a sudden turn for the worse – a fall off a ladder, a debilitating car accident, a stroke that has left them paralysed down one side, face skewed and confidence shattered. For now, hospital routines have taken over their lives, with timetables for physiotherapy, occupational therapy and psychology appointments pinned on a board next to their beds. I walk past small groups in common areas working on art projects, crutches propped beside them. I wait with Mum in queues for meals, other patients shuffling along in wheelchairs and walking frames. After a few days, it starts to feel normal. Mum makes her way to a table where people are familiar, smiles and says a tentative hello. People shuffle over to make room for her.

After her initial bewilderment, Mum begins to find the routines of the place comforting. We walk arm in arm down hallways, make our way to the kitchen and the lounge, and gradually venture further and further around the hospital. Eventually, the physiotherapist gives Mum permission to walk outside. We wander slowly around the hospital's sensory garden, set up by one of the nurses to help people with head injuries recover. Various sections extend out from a large golden ash. Mum is besotted with the water feature that gurgles in one corner; she laughs at a gaggle of clay ducks that surprises us as we round a bend. She delights in touching and smelling the herbs. While the garden is very different to her own, it is familiar, comforting. I see her visibly relax for the first time in weeks.

—

My brother and I sit with Mum in speech therapy sessions, and smile as an enthusiastic young therapist says over and over *siga siga* (slowly, slowly). It will be the mantra that defines their relationship over the coming months. Slow down. Take your time. *One word at a time.*

As Mum starts making progress, the question we keep asking is: 'When can Mum go home?' We are told it's likely she will need to keep having speech therapy for several months.

After a few weeks, just when it looks as if we might be nearly there, the occupational therapist tells me that, when asked to make toast, Mum stuck a knife in the toaster to get it out. 'Does she live with someone? What supports are available for her at home?' They are concerned for her safety.

We meet with the hospital psychologist, who tells Dennis and I that we need to be mindful of Mum getting depressed, which is a common side-effect of strokes. She tells us that Mum is making good progress. Her appetite is good, she is active, and she is grieving her losses in a completely appropriate way. As each day passes, I admire my mother more – her resilient spirit, her ability to deal with life's blows. Finally, her team agrees that with supervision she is at least ready to go home for a weekend.

—

Dennis and I fret when we arrive to pick her up and Mum is nervous. Will we cope? What if something happens when Dennis is asleep? We've quickly become used to the security of 24-hour nursing care, the comfort of institutional routines and supports. Now we are on our own again.

—

When Mum enters the front door of her home several weeks after she left in an ambulance, she is teary, her step over the threshold tentative. She makes her way around the kitchen, looks up at the myriad icons and crosses herself automatically. Next, she grabs a knife from the kitchen drawer. Dennis and I look on, eyes wide. Mum walks out the back door, down the step and straight into the garden. As she climbs into the raised garden bed I stand next to her, ready to catch her if she topples over, as if she is a toddler. Expertly, she begins cutting the newest shoots of broccoli, waves her arm for me to go and get a plastic bag. Instinct, a lifetime of habit, has set back in. For the first time in weeks, I feel that everything is going to be okay. Our mother is back home where she belongs. And even though it's only for the weekend, it's a start.

Several days later, Mum comes back home to stay. There's a whirlwind of visits from occupational and speech therapists, regular doctor and hospital visits. There are daily challenges that leave Mum frustrated and upset: she can't remember how to dial a phone number or read, has forgotten how to cook basic dishes, is confused about where things are in her kitchen. Her therapists assure us that at least some skills and language will come back – but slowly. Dennis and I have daily telephone conversations to coordinate her care, and debrief. He has become her full-time carer, feels concerned about leaving her on her own. I try and give him some respite so that he can get out, go for a run, watch a movie. Slowly, we ease back into some sort of routine.

Though I am still spending every spare moment with Mum, my own life returns to some semblance of order. As if returning from a dream, I see from my long list of unread emails that my writing group is due to meet. Though I'm tired, I make an effort to go. They ask after Mum, and it feels good to debrief about the last manic month. As a group, we have been meeting at a pub every six weeks for over a decade, and there have been many stories to share in that time – personal crises and creative milestones, ill health and the death of a few close friends. Much of the time, it feels more like a support group than a writer's group. I mention that a trip to Ikaria feels even more elusive now with Mum's ill health. They encourage me to keep the spark alive despite the challenges.

Fellow group member and friend Sam texts a few weeks later: 'Jamie Oliver on television now – in Ikaria!' I leave the sink, where I am scrubbing pots and switch on the television. And there's Jamie, with camera crew in tow, cooking up a feast with Ikarian islanders as he makes his way around Blue Zones locations. Jamie is looking much trimmer than I remember him, and I wonder if it's a happy side effect of putting into place some of the practices of the world's longest-lived peoples. I watch, amused, as he tries to outdo Maria the matriarch when making dough for herb and spinach pies. There is no competition – Maria wins hands down. I want so much to join them as they sit around the table, three generations of Ikarians and Jamie Oliver, eating pies and drinking the local brew. But Mum needs me now and I'm about to start a new job teaching – once again, the time is not right.

At any rate, the segment reminds me that I am lucky enough to have already been shown how to make pies by my octogenarian friend, *Theia* Georgia. On her outdoor garden table, she showed me how to roll out homemade pastry with a broom stick. When it was the size of a large disc, she patiently pulled at the edges, until it looked like a translucent tablecloth. She cut this in squares and layered it across several trays, which she filled with a mixture of chopped greens, herbs, feta and eggs. This she covered with pastry. She made many such pies in one batch, and would give these to neighbours and friends. She still makes them, despite being in her mid-eighties.

Enthused, I defrost some pizza pastry that George prepared last week. There's a bunch of spinach in the fridge, some mint in the garden. I wash it, let it dry. In the morning, I will chop it, and mix it with eggs and feta to make improvised pies to take to Mum's for lunch. It feels good to offer her something that I've made with my own hands, inspired by competent elders Maria and Georgia.

Teaching

After the last manic few weeks with Mum, I barely have time to take stock before starting my new job teaching. There's lots to do: preparing for new classes; in-house training; meeting students; negotiating educational administrative systems. These are all new things to me. My colleagues are patient and understanding, often asking how Mum is, empathising with any small challenges I describe. I feel like I am flying by the seat of my pants, not having had as much time to prepare as I would have liked. But despite this, I feel well supported, which helps me cope with all the new things I must learn. I am alert. My mother is slowly on the mend and I have an exciting new job.

A few weeks in, my colleague Jacqui and I are teaching students the craft of writing immersion essays. When we introduced the concept of immersing themselves in a new experience and writing about it, some of the students got excited about the extreme things they might do – stop eating food altogether, go out clubbing all night, take lots of drugs.

Jacqui and I looked at each other, our mothering instincts coming to the fore. 'Don't do anything that will put you in danger …'

At the start of the semester, I knew very little about each student except for those we'd been told would need special consideration. One has anxiety and panic attacks, another Asperger's syndrome. Someone else is afflicted with chronic depression.

Their essays fill in the gaps and suddenly they become more than their ailments – they have parents and siblings, interests and passions, desires and fears. I am reminded yet again of the privilege of being let into people's lives, of hearing their stories, being allowed to wind and meld them into the pastiche of my own life.

I'm reading a student's work as he looks on expectantly. He describes himself running in the back streets of Preston, trying to avoid stepping in dog shit. The early morning hush transports him, reminding him of walking with his mother in Ocean Grove. The rain comes down and the stitch he's expecting doesn't materialise ...

'Is it any good?' he asks when I've finished.

'It's very evocative. You've got some great imagery, a good eye for detail. Perhaps you could tweak this a little here ...'

Among the awkward first drafts, the ill-formed sentences and the spelling mistakes, there are nuggets of beauty in all the students' stories – an amusing interaction with a sibling, the feel of rain on hot skin, a surprising conversation with a stranger. We find that a disengaged young man who spends most of his class time watching and tittering at YouTube clips has a dark sense of humour and a talent for writing snappy dialogue. The quiet woman at the back of the class makes us salivate with her vivid description of a shared family meal.

One afternoon while all the students are busy working on their essays, Jacqui and I turn to each other.

'I've got a new book for you. You'll love this,' says Jacqui, handing over another novel, which I swap for the one I have for her. In the few months that we've been teaching together, we've discovered a shared love of reading, our tastes surprisingly similar. During this time, we've waxed lyrical about the evocative landscape in Hannah Kent's *Burial Rights*, argued feverishly about the merits and downfalls of Hanya Yanagihara's *A Little Life*, and broken down the elements of Liane Moriarty's *Big Little Lies*.

While talking to Jacqui, I'm reminded of a conversation I had with friends in high school about what we wanted to do with our lives.

'Imagine being paid to read and write books,' I had said wistfully. I think how important books have been in my life, I spent hours at the local library as a teenager, escaping into worlds that I couldn't have imagined, rejoicing in others' words, discovering new ideas and stepping into the shoes of characters with lives far from my own. As a surly teenager, I would lie in bed for hours on end reading, while Mum grumbled for me to get up and help her in the kitchen.

Now, as a writer, I hanker to create something meaningful, beautiful, perhaps something that will make a difference. It took a long time for me to arrive at this point – I became a social worker first, working in various health education roles for over a decade – but the need to write, to express myself through words, to tell my story and those of others, never went away. I took the leap of leaving my salaried job several years ago to start a writing business and to have more time to write creatively.

The risk has paid off. Now I write for a living. I teach others to do the same. And I'm surrounded by people who share a passion for stories. I've finally found my calling. As Jacqui and I run into Nic in the corridor and stop to have a chat, I experience a happy sense of having arrived, of having found *my people*. Now that I've got my sociable corridor discussions, I couldn't be happier.

—

It's Sunday morning, and the kids are still asleep. George is out in the backyard, watering the garden. I'm in the kitchen, savouring the quiet while I create meals from the offerings in my fridge and pantry. I enjoy the feeling of making something from seemingly not much at all, the unhurried improvisation and the sense of satisfaction that comes from knowing I have cooked a few things for the week when I will have less time.

I move between the lima beans bubbling on the stove, and the vegetables in the sink waiting to be washed and trimmed. As I'm chopping and grating and slicing I sink into a reverie, a meditation of sorts. Thoughts float in and out of my head and I think about the week ahead.

I need to finish marking essays, I should book a follow-up GP appointment for Mum, and it would be good to call my cousin, Kathy, who I haven't spoken to in a while. I stop and add some points to my running list of things to do. Now that I've cleared my mind, I can afford to get creative.

I'm not quite sure what might result from the ingredients on the bench and stove, but I'm thinking we will have beans in a spicy sauce and a finely grated coleslaw salad wrapped in wholemeal Lebanese pita bread. So long as they kids haven't filled up on snacks, they are willing to try most things that I cook. The beans and salad will carry over to dinner, accompanied by the snapper that George picked up yesterday. He'll bake this with some olives, tomatoes and zucchini. We should have enough leftovers for our lunches tomorrow. Some of the cooked beans will go into the freezer and I can add them to a stew during the week.

I've been trying to think like an Ikarian *yiayia* when it comes to stocking up, even though we have a range of food shops within a kilometre of our home. I've been more conscious of having enough staples in the pantry so I don't have to head out to the shops as often – so I've been spending less and avoiding impulse buys. Dried and canned pulses and legumes, rice, couscous and quinoa, passata and canned tomatoes, eggs, olive oil and dried herbs are now rarely absent from the pantry or the fridge. From these, along with whatever vegetables are in the crisper, I can usually create something my family will eat. George and I might supplement these with a nice piece of fish we've picked up from the local fishmonger, a few chicken thigh fillets or some lamb shanks.

It's a challenge feeding a family every day, and the aisles at our local supermarket are still doing a good job of trying to seduce me with their pre-prepared wares – meat that has already been marinated, rice that has been parboiled, pizza that only requires twelve minutes of heating on the cardboard tray it comes on, meals that come in a plastic container that just require a zap in the microwave. Even now, I'm very tempted by these things, but one look at the long list of ingredients – some of which I can't identify and many of which are added sugars, salt and fats – and I force myself to put them back. *Yiayia* simply wouldn't approve.

It's getting more challenging to find good things to eat at the supermarket, so I have widened the net, shopping more at the Asian, Italian and Greek food stores not far from home. At the Asian grocery, ten dollars buys me enough vegetables and tofu for a substantial and quick stirfry. At the Greek deli, the same amount buys me enough dried beans to last a month. At the Italian greengrocer, I might land several kilos of stone fruit in season, keeping my voraciously hungry teenage son in snacks for a few days. In the absence of flavoured rice crackers and chocolate biscuits, he eats plums and bananas. And though he still complains that there is 'nothing to eat', he seems to have a snack in his hand every time I see him.

I think back to the boxes of fruit my parents used to buy from the markets in summer and early autumn – a box of grapes, a whole watermelon, a tray of passionfruit that we would finish in a matter of days. Eating a hunk of cool watermelon on a hot day and trying to spit the pips as far as possible is one of my fondest childhood memories.

The beans are almost ready when I hear the kids starting to stir. George comes in from the garden and says he'll cook some eggs. He has just brought in the first of the silverbeet from the garden, and a few stalks of thyme. I pull some crusty homemade bread from the freezer to accompany the eggs and greens. It's still early in the morning, but George and I have got breakfast, lunch and dinner covered. Now we can get on with our day.

—

Emmanuel and I are sitting at the kitchen table one afternoon after school. When I'm home, I make a concerted effort to sit down with the kids to touch base about their day, even if it's only for a short time. Offering something delicious helps to keep my son sitting and talking – today it's leftover lamb.

'What does it all mean, Mum?' Emmanuel asks.

'What does *what* mean?'

'Life.'

'Mmm, that's a question that people have been asking for a long time ...'

'You're born, you go to school, you get a job, buy a home, maybe have kids, get old, and then you die.' He says it all really fast.

'Yes, I can see how you might think about it like that,' I say carefully. 'But you're forgetting all the stuff in between. Lots of people think there's more after you die, that you go to a higher place. Like a continuum. And other people think this is it – one life.'

'What do *you* think?' asks Emmanuel.

'It's reassuring to think that there is something more, but how would I know?' I say. 'Mostly I think we should make the most of the time we have. Try and be good to each other rather than worry too much about what will come next. Enjoy the little things – like you and me sitting here having this leftover lamb, and talking about life.'

He frowns. 'I worry that that's all there is. It feels like you work for things, and then what? It all has to end.'

'I know that's sad. Perhaps that's why some of us have children – so that it doesn't end. Maybe you'll have your own children one day, and enjoy teaching them things, and looking after them.'

'I don't know ...' says Emmanuel.

'It's easier if you don't jump forward too much, or even backwards. Try and enjoy what you have right now.'

Emmanuel nods, but I can tell he is still thinking about it. Is it natural for a teen to worry about the meaning of life? I wonder. Then I figure it's probably as good a time as any to be considering these things – he's about to launch into young adulthood. And I'm glad we're talking about it.

'Is there any more lamb? It's good.'

I get up, reheat the last of the lamb and divvy it up between us, giving Emmanuel the larger serving. In the last few years, he has grown more than two feet. I still can't get used to him stooping to give me a kiss, or his adolescent limbs taking up so much space. We dig in, wiping the lemony juices at the bottom of the plate with the bread George made. I try to take my time, savouring the taste. I look at my sensitive son expectantly, waiting to see if he has any more big questions.

'Thanks, Mum. Is there anything else to eat?'

—

A few days later, Mum, Dennis and I go to church. While Mum is doing remarkably well following her stroke, she no longer feels confident going to church by herself. I can tell Mum is pleased that I have come. We are here for the funeral of a former neighbour in his late eighties who passed away recently. We've come to honour his memory. I greet his wife, *Theia* Georgia, and she hugs me tightly. She too is glad we are here.

We are surrounded by the smell of incense and perfume. The cantors chant rhythmically. High above, mournful Byzantine saints look down protectively. I remember being a child, wondering if God might literally speak to me in church, give me a sign that He was real. As the service droned on, and He didn't speak, I would fidget, step from foot to foot, unable to stay still. Eventually, I would complain of feeling faint, the cloying smells and bodies making me feel uneasy. Mum would sigh and begrudgingly take me outside.

As I've gotten older, I find the rituals of the church more comforting: the chanting that gives me a chance to still my thoughts for a time; and the regular commemorative services and communal meals that follow when someone dies – seven days, forty days, six months, a year; the chance to see people who I might not otherwise see. The ancient and familiar symbolism of biers, candles and naively painted icons is reassuring. It feels good to step out of my day-to-day life for a brief time and let my mind wander in such an environment.

The priest reflects on the life of the deceased, and tells us that while we might now be sad that he has passed, his spiritual life continues in heaven – life is a continuum, and the body is but a mere temporary vessel. I listen with interest, unable to make myself believe that there is anything more after we pass on. Still, I am surrounded by people who are familiar to me, people who I have grown up with, and I'm glad to be here at this moment.

—

The summer holidays come around yet again and I'm in the laundry, piling towels into the washing machine, when Emmanuel says, 'Mum, I think you're going deaf. It takes you ages to answer me.'

I don't dignify his comment with an answer, infuriating him further.

'See, that just proves my point,' he grumbles.

Emmanuel has been complaining of my ailing hearing for some months now. He doesn't get the quick responses he expects when he tells me his pressing news, asks his very important questions, talks about his wonderful ideas. More and more, I find myself having to drag myself from my thoughts to focus on what the rest of the people in the house are saying, stop what I am doing and turn to face them, so I can hear them. Disconcertingly, I've noticed I sometimes have to get my students to repeat things. But it's not enough to make me go to the doctor to get my hearing checked out. That might be inviting something in that I'm not ready for.

While I've been taking Mum to the doctor regularly for blood pressure and cholesterol check-ups and enjoy the time it gives us to sit and chat while we wait, I avoid visiting the doctor myself. I dislike the feeling of something being wrong with me – I feel like it implies a weakness, a loss of control. Thankfully, apart from the odd migraine, I haven't been sick for the past few years, not even with a small cold. I've only been to the doctor once since that day I followed the swishy-skirted GP to her office. By way of follow-up, my regular doctor took the requisite blood tests a year after that visit and everything was in order. By that time, I'd lost several kilos, my blood sugar levels were normal, my cholesterol levels were healthy and my iron levels acceptable. He didn't bat an eyelid. I didn't tell him about my Ikarian-inspired path to better health – our fifteen minutes were already up by then.

Today my body feels good. I'm moving around a lot every day. I'm eating well most of the time, if a little too much. I'm sleeping well. Drinking moderately. I've kept most of the weight off. In my daily routines, I've become more social. I'm perhaps halfway through my life, all being well. One or two generations ago, I would have been considered 'old'. Ageing doesn't fill me with dread in the same way it did a few years ago. I'm getting used to being the age I am. I realise with a start that I'm feeling younger now than I did a few years ago.

But Emmanuel thinks differently. A few weeks ago, he flopped down on the couch beside me and started chatting as if I wasn't in the middle of reading my book. A few moments later, he stopped short, took a good look at me and frowned.

'Mum, you're getting wrinkles. That makes me sad. I don't want you to get old.'

I put my book down. 'We're all getting older. That's natural. You're getting older too.'

'I miss being a child.'

'You're barely out of childhood! And anyway, you can always be a child. It's all about how you feel in here.' I point to his chest. 'Sometimes *I* feel like a child,' I say crossing my eyes and pulling a face. He laughs. Goes away. I pick up my book, re-focus.

If I had a choice, I wouldn't choose for my body to age. I wouldn't choose for my belly to sag, or my skin to droop, or my muscles to wane. I don't think my mother would choose to lose her capacity to speak clearly, or my mother-in-law to stoop as she goes about her chores, slowly, painfully. All we can do is make the most of where we are at any given time.

—

A few weeks later, the kids go back to school. After nearly two months of having them at home every day, I relish having the days back to myself. I review my to-do list and realise that some of my 'self-care' tasks have been at the bottom of the list for several months now. My pap test is a few months overdue, and I haven't had an eye test for four years. Fortuitously, there's an opportunity to have a hearing test without the indignity of asking my doctor for it. My gym is offering them for free, according to a flyer on the back of their toilet door. I make sure to put the date in my diary.

When I go to the doctor for a pap test I ask for a female GP. While she takes the sample, we talk about parenting teenage kids. As she palpates my breasts, we talk about private versus public schools. As she takes my pulse, we talk about the importance of being there for our kids as they navigate these difficult teenage years, and the challenges of balancing work and family. Overall, it's an affirming visit. Everything is as it should be for my age. She leaves me with information about free mammograms. While it's a little too early for the government to invite me to have a free test, I can elect to invite myself. I thank her and promise myself I'll make an appointment.

A few days later, I knock off the optometrist visit. She says my eyesight has changed a little, but it doesn't warrant getting stronger reading glasses, especially as I don't wear the ones I already have.

'You can't afford to leave your next appointment so long next time. Things change a bit more quickly as you get older,' she says in parting.

I walk away with a spring in my step. Eyes: check. Boobs: check. Fanny: check. Now, for my hearing.

When the day of the hearing test arrives, I do a dance class, and then make my way to the gym carpark. The hearing van is there, as advertised, glistening in the sunshine. I approach apprehensively, wondering if I'll be in the company of much older people; if this is the day that I find out I need a hearing aid. A parent is there with a young child, another woman in gym gear just like myself. They take little notice of me. A nurse comes, and without taking my details, leads me into a padded cubicle, where I don some headphones and start the hearing tests. A few minutes later, they're done. The nurse shows me a range of dots on a graph. They sit at the top of the page. What does it mean?

'You have the hearing of a teenager. It's excellent,' she says.

'Really? My son thinks I have terrible hearing.'

'Teenagers are notorious for mumbling. And it's common for busy mums to have a lot on their mind – thinking about dozens of things at once. It probably takes you a while to focus on what he is saying.'

I could kiss this nurse person. I'm not going deaf. I can't wait to get home and gloat. I'm going to tell Emmanuel he needs to *e-nun-ci-ate*. And to learn to say, 'Excuse me.' I walk out into the sunshine, smiling. I've got ears like a teenager and all my bits are in good working order. I feel young. Very young.

Rejoicing

'It would have been a year since your Mum's stroke. We'll book the house for then. It will be a celebration. We can cut a cake …'

My cousin Kathy has had yet another win – this time a voucher to stay in a family-sized cabin at a caravan park. Ever-generous, she wants to treat her two younger sisters Dim and Georgia, myself and our two mothers to a 'girls' weekend away with her.

We agree that it's going to be hard to get Kathy's mum to come. My aunty Sophia spends a lot of time at home, avoiding social functions.

Kathy frowns. 'If my mum doesn't come, yours won't either.'

'I'll work on mine, and you work on yours,' I say. 'Let's talk in a few days.'

By the time I ring my mother, she has already spoken with my aunt.

'My sister doesn't want to come. And anyway, what will George say that you're going away, leaving him with the kids?'

'They're his kids too, Mum,' I reply. 'George is perfectly capable. And anyway, Kathy won the accommodation, we'll bring food, it won't cost a thing …' Mum hates it when we spend our money on what she considers frivolities, especially if those frivolities involve spending money on her.

'Still. Your aunt won't come.'

But my mother has underestimated my cousin's persuasive

skills. Kathy tells her mum that we are lucky to still have her sister with us, well and healthy one year after her stroke; and does she remember that one year ago, they had all rushed to the emergency department, thinking they were losing their beloved Chrysoula? She tells her mum she owes it to her sister to come away with us. A little emotional blackmail always works.

And so, a date is set and a caravan park booked on the Mornington Peninsula, across the road from a beach. In the weeks leading up to our getaway, emails fly back and forth between us cousins – who will bring what food, who will carpool with whom, what time we can get away. Between us we have twelve children and it's not easy to coordinate their care. Some of the older kids agree to look after the younger ones. Husbands step in.

Finally, the day arrives when we can go.

We meet at our house. We cut the cake. Mum starts crying. This past year hasn't been easy. She's been frustrated as small improvements have been hard earned, each word and phrase that resurfaces from the depths of memory sorely won. Her speech is still somewhat garbled, she still struggles with names, but she has come a long way. She hasn't stopped trying to talk to us, hasn't withdrawn, laughs through the challenges. She still has long phone conversations with both of her sisters every day, even if they talk more than she does. She walks with Dennis for more than an hour each day, tends her garden, has learnt to cook again. Her trademark optimism, humour and spirit are never far away. There is much to celebrate. We sit around her, these loud, outspoken women who love her; wipe away her tears, hug and reassure her.

After loading the last of our things into the car, we're off. I realise it's the first time my cousins and I have taken our mothers away together. Going away for a weekend is foreign to Mum and her sisters. It was not something they did with their husbands or families. It feels like we're taking two kids out for a treat. The tables have turned, and not for the first time I find myself feeling like I'm mothering my own mother.

When we arrive, we unload the food. While we loosely agreed on who would bring what, we've overcatered and the junk food pile is like a mountain. Will I be able to resist its charms?

Even though we have so much food, that evening someone wants fish and chips, and someone else wants pizza. We go for a walk along the beach, dipping our feet in the water, slowly making our way to the strip that boasts countless fast-food franchises. Eating decent food is going to be near impossible; I resign myself to a weekend of excesses.

Back at the caravan park, we overindulge and then loll about on the couches. Kathy has bought cosmetic face masks and little slippers we can wear to exfoliate our feet. She gets to work massaging and plumping, wiping away product with several little face towels she thought to bring. At the end of the night, I force her to lie down and give her a long face massage. She moans with pleasure.

When we were growing up, my cousins and I spent every spare minute in each other's company, walking to each other's homes a few suburbs away on weekends, sleeping at each other's houses. Now we see each other less often, mostly on social occasions. It's nice to be together again. While we are older, have responsibilities and have experienced quite a few challenges, it's not hard to revert to our childish ways, even if it's just for the weekend. It's a chance to catch up, talk more about where each of us is at, laugh at silly things.

Dim has a new job as a carer at a nursing home. After bringing up six kids as a full-time mum for many years, she is excited to be working and getting paid for it. She is good at her job and seems to instinctively know what each of her patients need.

In keeping with my interest in the Ikarians and what it takes to live well for longer, I ask her what we should do now that will help us to grow old well later.

Dim doesn't hesitate in her response. 'Don't gain too much weight. It's really challenging for those who are very large. They can't move, everything hurts. We shift them from their beds to their chairs on a harness and I feel for them – it must be so undignified.

'Stay social – even the people who are very sick, if they come to the common room and talk to people, they do better than the ones who stay in their rooms all day. They're the ones more likely to be depressed.

'And keep moving if you can. I had one patient who passed away just recently – she was coming to my exercise class until a few days before she died. She had spirit, wouldn't give up.'

What Dim says affirms for me, yet again, what I've learnt from the Ikarians and what my Mum keeps teaching me each day. I think back to what VicHealth's Jerril Rechter said about investing today in your health future. I think I'm doing alright, mostly eating well, moving each day, and prioritising my connections with people, even if tonight the salty charms of the potato chips are having their way with me. I've come a long way from a few years ago, when I was lacking energy, and often felt at bit lost and flat. I still feel these things occasionally, but know now to be kind to myself during these times, to pick myself up by doing the things and seeing the people who make me feel good.

The next day, we take another slow walk along the beach. Our mothers walk arm in arm, barefoot, laughing and talking. Watching them, I'm so glad we convinced them to come.

On the last night, Dim, Georgia and I prepare a vegetarian pasta dish and a spinach salad. I fill my plate with salad and eat a small amount of pasta slowly. I've had my excessive hit of salty, fatty food, and have started to feel sluggish, uncomfortable. My body is telling me it's had enough. It's time to get back on track.

—

Since 'meeting' the Ikarians, I find myself noticing older people more. On trains, at parties, even at seminars. Sometimes I find myself asking outright, 'What does it take to live well, and long?' It's disingenuous, perhaps even a bit rude, but the response has always been enthusiastic.

The first time I asked the question, I was on a train sitting next to an impeccably dressed older man wearing a scarlet silk tie. In his hand, he held a brochure about The Ghan. I had a choice. I could surf the internet on my phone, or start a conversation. I started a conversation.

'Are you thinking of taking a trip?' I asked.

'Yes, I think my wife might like it.'

He then began talking about all the trips he had made in his life for his work, and about the ones he would like to take with his wife. Now that he had more time, he wanted to make the most of it.

On his lap rested a thick tome. He said he was going to teach himself Latin from scratch. After I finished a call with Dolores ('Mum, can you please pick up something yummy to eat?'), the man confessed that he didn't own a mobile phone. His wife was badgering him to get one, but he wouldn't give in. Whatever happened to him while he was out, happened. So be it. His tips for living long and well? Keep learning, walk every day and enjoy each moment. He got off the train and strode away at a brisk pace.

A few weeks later I had a long chat with a 91-year-old man at a party who still mowed his own lawn. He said he kept his mind active by regularly visiting the 'elderly' in a Jesuit nursing home, where he had existential conversations about the meaning of life. His advice on what it takes to live long, and well? Keep your mind and body active, be social, and make sure to marry a good woman. He took his wife by the arm and they climbed down the steps of my friend's house, steady as you please.

Today I met a 95-year-old woman at a writer's event. And so, I reeled out the question again, even before we had been properly introduced.

She didn't hesitate before answering.

'A good posture,' she said giving me a piercing look, as if to say, 'Are you listening to me?' I held my shoulders back as far as they would go, noticing she was standing ramrod straight.

'Have fun. Lots of it. I ate, drank, smoked, had sex. Have lots of sex if you can get it ...' she continued, her eyes twinkling. 'And be sure to let go of anger. Don't waste time being angry. Sometimes it's hard. You can't help it. But anger isn't worth it.'

Feasting

Our old brown kitchen is being taken apart piece by piece, its bulky brown mass being placed into the back of a trailer. Even though I have complained about its crooked cupboards, its poorly sealed sink and stovetop and its '70s-inspired colour, part of me is sad to see it go. *Her* go. I can't help but think of her as an old dame. A little tawdry, well worn, life battered, but a dame regardless. I've found myself keeping her extra clean the last few weeks, almost wanting to apologise that I haven't quite appreciated her enough. I realise now that she has served us well over the last decade since we've been in this home.

I think about how I have spent so much time in her, angsting about what to put in the many hundreds of lunchboxes I've packed for my children; preparing slow-cooked roasts with lemony potatoes for countless family meals in her rickety old oven with the wonky hinges. I remember Dolores and I spilling food colouring on her resilient old surfaces as we tried to reproduce cakes from the Women's Weekly *Birthday Cake Book*; George has kneaded hundreds of bread loaves on her strong back; and Emmanuel cut his culinary teeth in her hardy griller by making cheese sandwiches that invariably left their oily footprint all over her. She took it all without so much as a whimper.

The next day, Phil the cabinetmaker arrives first thing in the morning to install our new kitchen. Even before he's put his tools down, I've got the kettle going.

'Have you had breakfast? Would you like a cuppa?' I ask.

Despite having packed away all our utensils and cups in antic-ipation of the new kitchen going in, my inner Greek host can't help herself. I feel compelled to offer sustenance, just like my mother and grandmother before me. In Mum's case, any work-men who came to do a job would be offered a sit-down luncheon meal, often with crumbly shortbread biscuits or honeyed cakes to follow. In Mum's village, she tells me that helpers who came to harvest olives or help till the soil could always expect to be fed, no matter how poor the host. Often the workers were not paid, but they could always count on a meal.

'Just a cuppa would be great. Coffee. White. No sugar please,' says Phil as he downs his toolbox.

After finding some instant coffee in a box, I apologise that I don't have any biscuits to offer him.

'Don't worry about it. I stopped saying yes to sweets when I do jobs,' he says. 'When I reached 100 kilos, I decided it was time to start saying no.'

I raise my eyes, surprised. Phil looks slim and fit. I ask him how long he's been doing this job.

'Nearly forty years. More than twenty years with this com-pany,' he replies. 'I can't complain. I like my job. The sun is shining. And I'm alive.' He smiles widely. It's only 7.30 in the morning and I'm wondering where Phil gets his energy from.

He eyes the job in front of him. 'Your floor is very crooked.'

'Is it going to be a problem?' I ask, alarmed. I've been hanker-ing for this new kitchen for so long I don't want it to be lopsided.

'It's a First World problem. It'll be alright once I've had a cigarette.'

I follow him out with my cuppa. I'm a story addict and I have a feeling I'm going to get my fix this morning.

He asks me what I do, and I tell him I'm a writer and a teacher.

'I write websites, reports, that sort of thing. That's what helps pay the mortgage. But I also write books.' I shrug almost apologetically, as if that's not a real job.

'Writing is my passion. Perhaps I'll write a book sharing the secret about how to live to a hundred!' I add, watching for his response. I've starting gauging people's reaction to how they feel about living a long time.

He pulls a face, as if to say that the idea doesn't appeal to him much at all. 'Better to have seventy good years than live to a hundred and feel miserable. My father is eighty-six. When he was eighty, his doctor said he should cut down on the fags, not drink so much. I said to him, "Dad, if you want to have half a bottle of wine with dinner, go for it." My mum is still whipping around the garden. If she gets tired, she sits on her push chair. It's all about quality, not quantity.'

He points to his heart. 'I've got a machine in there. I'd be dead without it. When I was diagnosed with cardiomyopathy a few years ago, they gave me three months to live. It shook me up, but it didn't stop me from doing anything. It was my own fault.' He holds up the cigarette. 'But I still rocked up to work each day. And I'm still here now.'

I smile, tempted to say he might give up the cigarettes, but I have a feeling Phil has heard it all before.

Sure enough, he grins as if he knows what I want to say. 'I'm not giving up the fags and the booze. I did get sick of being fat though. That I had to change. I threw the crap food out of the pantry, stopped eating the Tim Tams at night. If it's not in front of you, you won't eat it. I mean, you don't want to take it to extremes. *You can't eat this, you can't eat that.* That's boring. For me it was easy. I decided to say no every time someone offered me food on the job. It's been two years now and the weight has come off without even trying, without going on stupid diets ...'

Phil takes a final puff of his cigarette, drowns the last of his coffee and goes back into the kitchen to grapple with the crooked floor.

—

The next day, Emmanuel asks, 'When are we going to have noodles?'.

'It might be a bit hard to cook noodles without a working stove,' I reply. The electrician still needs to come. The countertop still needs to be put in. We won't have a functional kitchen for a few weeks yet.

'Not your noodles. The ones from the shop. You keep promising.'

Somehow the noodles from the take-out down the road are more alluring than the garden variety I cook at home. I suspect it has something to do with the copious amounts of oil, sauces and MSG the shop adds. And the fact that I add tons of vegetables to my noodle dishes.

We've had no sink or indoor stove these last few days. George and I wash dishes in a bucket outside and we've set up the camping stove to cook on. But with Emmanuel's soccer on tonight, I can't get my head around cooking. I cave. Bring on the MSG.

Our closest shopping strip offers more than a dozen take-away options, despite its small size. Dolores and George choose to have fish and chips. Emmanuel has his favourite noodle dish and I order a vegetable noodle soup which is so salty I can't finish it. Instead I nick chips from George's plate. We decide to watch what's on television, so we don't bicker about what movie to download. Somehow, it's easier to agree when there's not a lot of choice.

I spend most of the next day loading everything I packed into boxes back into the kitchen cupboards – and realise that we probably only use a quarter of them. I put aside the three-dozen small Greek coffee cups (I can't imagine having that many people come to drink Greek coffee), cull the many party platters my Mum has passed on over the years, debate whether we need that awkwardly shaped apple corer that was advertised on one of the telemarketing shows.

Dolores helps me, rejoicing in throwing away all the miscellaneous cups, saucers and plates. There's something liberating about shedding and culling.

After we've finished, she offers to make pasta with pesto for dinner. I'm grateful to her – it's a relief to take a break from cooking. I try not to worry about the fact that we haven't eaten anything that vaguely resembles a vegetable today, or that this is the third time we're having pasta this week. Instead, I down a glass of wine, relieved that everything fits into our new kitchen.

The next day, we meet Mum and Dennis at Papa Gino's, our favourite pizza and pasta restaurant in Lygon Street. The first time George came here was when Dolores was three days old. He brought her here while I recuperated from surgery after her birth, drinking a glass of house wine and celebrating being a father over a spaghetti marinara. We've been coming as a family regularly ever since. Dolores prides herself on never having ordered anything other than gnocchi bolognese. It hasn't changed a bit over sixteen years and that's how she likes it. The owner greets George like an old friend and takes our order.

When the food arrives, it's clear we've over-ordered, what with two large pizzas, salad, a parmigiana that fills the whole plate, two bowls of pasta and drinks all round.

All the time we are eating, Mum worries. 'This is so much food. You've spent too much. Can I pay? I could have cooked at home, it wouldn't have cost you a cent ...'

'Mum, please. Just enjoy it,' I say.

Over dinner we do the usual when we go out – eat, laugh, tell stories, bicker, then eat some more.

We ask to have some of the food wrapped to take home and then make our way to Brunettis, a Melbourne institution, for coffee and sweets. There we order drinks and ice-cream, which Mum and George can't finish. I am not at all hungry, but pick at Mum's leftover ice-cream because I can't bear to see it go to waste. All the while Mum shakes her head. So much excess. So much money.

By now, I have to agree with her. We've parted with more than $150 and I feel sick.

The next day, I go shopping at our local greengrocer and stock up on vegetables, pulses and nuts. The bill comes to $100 – enough to feed the whole family for several days. I start preparing some vegetables to make a big batch of baked spring rolls. It's time to get back on track. Again.

—

In the early days of my infatuation with Ikaria, I subscribed to the Blue Zones newsletter and an alert for the latest update now pings in my inbox. I follow the link, which tells me it's okay to drink wine in moderation, and in company. It reminds me that the Ikarians drink their wine with a splash of water.

I do a quick mental calculation. It's been some two years since I read about the Ikarians. In the last year Mum has had a stroke and I've started a busy new job. Each member of the family has their own preoccupations – school, work, sport and various hobbies. The dinner table is our meeting ground most nights as we swap and share news about our day; argue and make up again. The last year has passed very quickly.

I see I have time to do the longevity test before I head off to work.

The test comes up with a life expectancy result of ninety-seven years. I smile. Eating well, moving lots and having small daily rituals for connection has become an integral part of my life. But despite the good result, something is still niggling at me.

As work has got busier and I've taken on more teaching, there's even less time to relax. Every minute is stretched to within an inch of its life. I've had a few migraines in the past few months. The idea of scheduling time in to calm down stresses me out. I've never been one to sit still for long.

I think back to the Ikarians and their laidback attitude to time. While I've come a long way, perhaps there is still more to be learnt from them. Now that Mum is doing so much better, and the kids are older, I wonder if the time has come to put the trip to Ikaria back on the agenda?

Later in the week, George and I take an evening walk. It's late summer, and a cool breeze offers some respite from the heat of the day.

Amid the comfortable banter about the kids, gardens and cleaning out the garage, I raise the topic of going to Ikaria again. George turns to me, looks at me searchingly.

'You need to do this, Spiri. Don't worry about us. We'll be alright. When do you think would be a good time?'

I hesitate. 'Um, I haven't thought that far. Are you sure? What about the kids? Work? You'll need to take some time off ...'

I'm not sure why I'm resisting this. I have George's blessing. And I know he and our children will be okay.

I suspect the only person standing in my way is me.

—

Over the coming weeks, our dinner conversations go back and forth about the logistics of how to make a trip to Ikaria happen – or rather, how the home fires might be stoked in my absence.

George tells me to stop fretting. In his mind, he has it all sorted. He says my responsibility is to go to Ikaria; his is to manage the home while I'm there. He will cut down his fulltime work to three days a week. Outsource one or two meals a week to the same company that delivers food to his parents. Maybe even get a cleaner. And by the way, how many loads of washing do I do each week?

On the one hand, I admire George's attitude – if he doesn't have the time to do it himself, then he will pay someone else to do it. Simple. But on the other hand, I can't help but be offended that the things I do each day might be outsourced so easily, paid for with the swipe of a credit card. That what I do for free someone else can do for money, without my emotional attachment to the rituals of our daily life

For their part, the kids baulk at the idea of outsourcing meals. Dolores offers to cook three times a week to avoid it. Emmanuel says he will cook once a week – he could do fried eggs, or perhaps grilled sandwiches. Dolores had looked at me as if to say, 'We'll survive, Mum, but hurry back.'

It's settled then. I'm going to Ikaria.

Preparing

My friend Angela's brother, Alex, has kindly offered to introduce me to a couple who live in Melbourne, but are originally from Ikaria. At Alex's suggestion, Sotiris and his wife, Vaso, have agreed to talk to me about the island and its people. This might help me to decide when to go, and where to stay.

Sotiris has a shock of thick white hair, chiselled features and huge light-coloured eyes that meet mine appraisingly. His stance is confident, and he gives the appearance of height, even though he is more stocky than tall. It's hard to tell how old he is.

We shake hands, his grip firm. I note his forearms are taut with muscle and have prominent veins, the arms of a labourer. I am not sure whether to speak in Greek or English, or whether to call him Sotiris, or use the more formal *Kirie*, Mr Sotiris. I think he falls somewhere between my age and that of my parents.

I end up introducing myself in Greek. *'Me lene Spirithoula.'*

'Welcome. Spiridoula, where are your parents from?' It's a question I've had from Greek-born Australians all my life.

They were from near Kalamata, I tell Sotiris.

'I was in the army in Kalamata, I got my first haircut there.' He smiles at the memory.

His wife, Vaso, comes up behind him. She is shorter and rounder that her husband. She kisses me warmly on both cheeks, welcomes me to their home.

We take a seat and Vaso heads off to the kitchen, saying she has just prepared us a small *meze*, a snack. She proceeds to bring out plate after plate: grilled mushrooms, cheese pie, dips, several different types of pickled vegetables, cheese and bread. After placing a bottle of ouzo and a canister of ice on the table, Vaso pours little shots for us and herself. Sotiris takes a beer.

Sotiris was born in Ikaria, Vaso in nearby Samos. They migrated to Australia more than forty years ago. They still travel to Ikaria every second year to visit their siblings and their parents, who are in their nineties. Sotiris finds a map of the island and points out where he grew up in the upper village of Therma, the site of Ikaria's hot springs.

We talk about his work in heavy construction, inserting metal rods into the concrete pillars of new apartments. He tells me he is sixty-seven but still manages to keep up with the young blokes.

When I ask about his early life in Ikaria, he replies: 'In my village, we grew everything. We even grew our own *lupines* (black-eyed peas) and lentils. We had our own animals for meat – hens, pigs, goats. We would sell the meat to the butcher to make a bit of money and we would just keep the entrails for ourselves. What could you do when you had very little money? We used the whole pig, everything except the bristles. Before we had a fridge, we would pickle the pork in fat and salt. We ate wild greens and herbs, grew our own fruit and vegetables.'

He shrugs. 'What can I say? The air was clean. There was no stress. It was a different lifestyle.'

He pulls out a calendar containing photos of the island, dated 2010. We flick through it, noting the beautiful beaches, the little churches and barren mountainsides. He shows me carefully framed photos of the island from 1913. A fridge magnet that says, 'Clocks and stress have no place in Ikaria.'

On a small map, he points to the windy roads that connect each village and town. 'There were no roads then like these ones now,' he says, tracing them with his finger. 'On the rare occasions when someone would come down to the main town from one of the inland villages, they looked wild. As a kid, I thought they were from another planet.'

I ask Sotiris and Vaso if they have any kids or grandkids, and Vaso pulls out a wedding book marking their daughter's wedding day. I flick through it, admiring the young bride and her entourage.

'You should show them our wedding album,' Sotiris says, 'it's huge!'

It takes me a few moments to realise he is joking, poking fun at the fact that at most they probably only have a couple of wedding photos. Times have changed. Sotiris came to Australia with a half-filled suitcase; his kids are growing up in relative comfort.

When I tell Sotiris I am considering going to Ikaria in the springtime, he pulls a face. 'It's still cold. You won't see as many people out. All the weddings happen in summer – by necessity they are outside, as there are no large indoor venues. Why don't you go in July? There are a lot of festivals on then. We'll be there. We'll show you around. We won't leave any stone unturned. It's very hard to get around without a car, if you don't know anyone ...'

He plies me with another serve of mushrooms.

I thank him and tell him I will think about it.

'And, don't tell the old people you're there to find out why they live a long time,' he continues. 'After they did research on longevity there, a few of the elders died. The other elders thought that the researchers had put the evil eye on them, and stopped talking about why they lived so well and so long.'

We all laugh. I promise to keep his advice in mind.

After we've exhausted the wedding album and depleted the *mezethes* (small bites), Alex and I get up to take our leave. Sotiris hands us a generous jar of honey from his own hives and passes his phone number on to me so I can let him know how I get on in Ikaria. 'And don't forget, if you want to come a bit later in the year, we'll leave no stone unturned ...'

—

Despite Sotiris's advice, I decide to visit Greece in May, when the flowers in the countryside are in bloom, the weather is mild, and tourists aren't yet out in hordes. My reasons are more practical too. I have a short break from teaching then and the fares and accommodation are cheaper, which means I won't need to draw down so much on the mortgage. And I'm in luck. My cousin's ex-wife, Isa, who lives in Greece, is going to join me for some of the time I am on the island. She says she will bring her friend Niki, who grew up there. It's nice to know I will have company.

Once again I serach the internet for Ikarian accommodation. It's been a little over two years since I came across Stamatis Moraitis on my computer. I've come a long way since then – I'm more comfortable in my skin; feel more content with my life each day; know when to take stock and curb the occasional 'spirit sickness'– a general malaise, a vague sadness and meaninglessness – when it strikes me. I no longer go to bed with indigestion more nights than I'd like to count. I'm feeling more connected to those around me – my kids, my husband, my mother, extended family and friends. And I'm doing more things in keeping with what is important to me and less of the things that aren't.

I find hotels overlooking azure blue water, glittering pools in the foreground, rustic hillside tavernas and rugged mountainsides. My guilt escalates. I'm wanting to find out how to live better, perhaps write something that will help others live better too, not to have a luxurious holiday.

'I'm going to miss you,' says Emmanuel, looking over my shoulder at the screen.

I stop what I'm doing and turn around. 'I'm going to miss you too.'

'They all look beautiful, Mum,' he says, nodding towards the places I've been looking at. 'Just book something.'

With just six weeks to go before I leave, I'm strangely hesitant about booking my fares or accommodation. I haven't even dug out my passport to check that it hasn't expired. There are so many things to think about – what to do about banking, buying a new suitcase, what pyjamas to take. It's easier to keep putting it off.

All the while, my life doesn't stop – a new bunch of students has started the year, I've got several business projects to complete, and I still need to cook and clean and get the kids to their activities.

It's been more than fifteen years since I've travelled overseas by myself and the thought of it makes me feel a little tired. And scared. The long flight. The transfers. Will I still remember how to negotiate taxis in Athens? How will I manage buses and bank tellers? What if I *die*?

Random and irrational worries swim around my head, but my main concern is how I will leave my family for a month. In the past, I've left them for a few days at a time, but never for this long. How will George manage the administration of family life, the little things like getting bills paid on time, getting the kids to their sporting commitments, answering the many questions each day that start with 'Mum …?' And most importantly, will the kids get their quota of vegetables each day?

Finally, with Emmanuel breathing down my neck, I find rooms at Thea's Inn in the tiny town of Nas on the southern side of the island. I read that Thea hosted the Blue Zones team when they stayed in Ikaria. Perhaps she can share with me her take on the longevity phenomenon. Before I can change my mind, I send her a message enquiring about a room for a few nights. After that, I will see what happens.

Emmanuel looks pleased. 'Good work, Mum. Can I come too?' he says with a smile.

What sort of mother leaves her family for a month to spend time in some obscure backwater where she has no family or connections?

My guilt makes me grumpy and irritable. I take it out on Emmanuel. *Just focus on your homework, stop making a mess, be nice to your sister ...* I am in overdrive trying to get him to curb his creative, scattered energy. Deep down I am worried that my sensitive young son might unravel in my absence. Or perhaps that I, without the stabilising influence of family, will myself become unwound.

As well as going to Ikaria, I'm planning to visit my relatives in Greece. I'm a bit apprehensive about the welcome I will get, concerned that I might be a burden. It's another way of convincing myself I'm making the wrong decision. I call my *Theia* Kanella and tell her tentatively that I am coming and that I'm hoping to spend a few days with her and my cousin, perhaps at the start of the trip.

'Does that work for you?' I ask.

Theia Kanella laughs. 'Everything works for us, Spiridoula.'

'I wish I could bring Mum. She would love it.' Mum speaks with family in Greece regularly, but hasn't visited since the 1970s.

'Can't you bring her?'

'It's hard for her to travel. She isn't the woman she once was ...'

'No, none of us are. None of us are,' Kanella says.

She puts me on to my cousin Stathis. I repeat my news, telling him I don't want them to go to any trouble on my part.

'You know I can live off those beautiful wild greens of yours.

A bit of cheese and bread and I'm a happy woman,' I say.

'Come, Spiridoula, and we will have a good time. There will be *horta*, and meat, and all sorts of things. We are rich in our hearts here and we will celebrate,' he says with characteristic pathos.

I laugh. Already I am looking forward to being among them, being a part of the simple rituals of cooking and eating together.

I share with Stathis my fears about something happening while I am away. I am worried that Mum might have another stroke, that she will slip away from us while I am many thousands of kilometres away.

'Spiridoula *mou*, I hope this doesn't happen,' he replies. 'But remember, our mothers, they have worked hard. Their bodies are tired. When the time comes for them to go, they will be ready. Maybe they are ready now.'

'*They* might be ready. But *I'm* not.'

He laughs a little sadly. 'They won't ask if you're ready. When the time comes, we need to let them go.' I know how close he is to his own mother. Despite teasing her mercilessly, I know he manages the home, loyally looking after *Theia* Kanella, whose rheumatoid arthritis and weak lungs often keep her bedridden for days at a time.

'Here, talk to your uncle,' I say to Emmanuel as he walks past.

Emmanuel looks abashed. His Greek is limited to a handful of phrases. *Euharisto.* (Thank you.) *Ohi yiayia, then thelo kiales patates.* (No, grandma, I don't want any more chips.) It's lucky Stathis's English is good.

Talking on the phone, Emmanuel starts laughing. I hear him assure Stathis that he will learn more Greek this year. Their conversation goes on and on, Emmanuel getting more garrulous as the minutes tick by.

When he passes the phone back, I ask Stathis what he said to Emmanuel. He laughs and says that some conversations are only to be held between men and tells me that I have an 'artist' on my hands in our young son.

'I should bring him with me to Greece. He would learn some more Greek,' I say.

'Why don't you?'

I hesitate. Despite my guilt, I know this is something I need to do on my own.

The start of May is only four weeks away, and my mind reels with all the things I need to do before then: finish this current teaching block and mark assignments, finalise projects and write reports, prepare for the trip, hand over the household reins to the rest of the family and make sure that everything is under control.

Meanwhile, family life keeps going. Dolores's books are spread across the kitchen table as she tries to study for the first of her Year 11 exams. George brings in the last of the cherry tomatoes and several huge pumpkins from our autumn garden, placing them in a pile in the hall. The seasons are oblivious to my distress – they keep rolling along as if nothing is happening.

Much to my chagrin, I wake up with a migraine and must take to my bed for the day. I ring work, down painkillers and force myself to sleep. In the early afternoon, propped up in my bed with a bowl of lentil soup, I realise that after all the Ikarians have taught me from afar – to eat food that makes my body feel good, to move more, to connect with those around me, to have a more generous spirit, I still need to learn to accept that there is only so much I can do in one day. I need to have a little more faith that the important things that need to get done, will.

Angsting

It's the Thursday before Easter and I'm rushing down our street on the way home from work, when I see my brother's car parked out the front of our house.

I make my way in, past hugs from Emmanuel, a kiss from Dolores, towards Mum and my brother. Mum has just put a large pot of fish and vegetable soup down on the stove, an oversized packet of toilet paper on the bench, and milk in the fridge.

'What have you brought this time?' I say, giving her a hug. 'One day you will come to our home empty-handed.'

'It's nothing. What do you want me to cook for Easter Sunday lunch?'

'There's no need to cook anything. I've got it covered,' I reply. Cooking has become harder for Mum since the stroke – she can't remember what goes in dishes she used to cook automatically, can't read recipes anymore, is easily flustered when she forgets where utensils are.

'Here, take some money and you can shop for something.' She puts some notes on the sideboard. I tell her off, but give up after a while. I know she will win the argument.

She starts to fossick in the cupboards for an apron. She's ready to start baking. When I told Mum I was going to make *koulouria* (traditional Easter cookies) with Dolores this year, she wanted to help. I was hoping she would say that, glad to harness her cooking expertise in a way that makes it easy for her. And I know it will make her feel useful.

A few days ago, when I was shopping for ingredients, I referred to a dog-eared Greek cookbook that my *Theio*, Uncle Spiro, gifted to Mum in the '70s, which is now mine. Inside the cookbook are several scraps of paper with recipes in Mum's writing, including 'Rena's *koulouria*'. I imagine Mum diligently jotting these down after tasting them at neighbours' or friends' houses. In Rena's recipe, Mum has listed the ingredients, but has omitted the method. I refer to a similar recipe in the cookbook, just in case she's forgotten the process. I don't want her to be embarrassed or stressed if she can't remember. Since the stroke, I find myself protecting her from things that might hurt or upset her. I'm conscious that her blood pressure can go up, and that this increases her risk of having another stroke.

'I'm just going to change out of my work clothes. I'll be right back, and we can start,' I tell her. She has found the flour and sugar, and is waiting impatiently for me to read out the amounts.

Dennis plans to go out while Mum, Dolores and I are baking. Before he leaves, he fills me in on the day's events.

'I went with Mum to the chemist today to fill a script. He took her blood pressure,' Dennis says.

'Was it okay?'

'Yeah, but he said she has an irregular heartbeat.'

I stop what I'm doing. 'An irregular heartbeat? It's only been a few weeks since we took her to the doctor. How can he tell that from a blood pressure monitor?' I ask.

'I don't know,' Dennis replies.

'Did he seem concerned?'

'He didn't say much. Just that we should check it out next time we go to the doctor.'

'Does he know she's had a stroke?'

'I don't think so.'

I turn to Mum. 'The chemist said something about your heart.'

'Oh that. That's nothing. Maybe because I took three of those tablets to help me sleep …' She's referring to the strong painkillers she has beside her bed.

'Three? All at once?'

She nods sheepishly.

'Mum, that's too much,' I say.

'The doctor said I can take as many as I like.' The doctor *had* said that the painkillers were less harmful than sleeping pills, which he didn't want to prescribe as he was concerned about Mum having falls during the night if she got up to go to the toilet.

'He said no such thing. I'm always with you when you go to the doctor.'

'Well, my sister said …'

'Mum! You can't just take any medication you like.'

'I know, but I can't sleep, and if I don't sleep, the next day, I can't talk properly. And then I worry about it.'

I can feel my own heart beating faster now, remembering Mum on a gurney, attached to monitors in emergency, me trying to take in what the doctors were telling me. A good amount of time has elapsed since then but the fear of it happening again hangs over our heads. Dennis looks concerned too.

Tomorrow is Easter Friday. I see the long weekend looming ahead, and fear the worst. What if Mum has another stroke, or a heart attack? And what if, knowing that there was a problem, I'd done nothing to help prevent it?

'I'm going to ring the pharmacist,' I say.

'Don't do that. We've got baking to do,' Mum protests.

'I don't care. Your health is more important than the *koulouria*.'

My voice is rising. I know I'm being a bit irrational, but I can't help it.

'There's nothing wrong with me. Let's just get on with it. I wish your brother hadn't said anything.'

I take myself off to my room and ring the pharmacist. No one picks up and I leave a message.

As we're mixing the ingredients for the *koulouria*, George comes home from shopping. He goes around the kitchen, blind-folding Dennis and the kids in turn to test whether they prefer the cheap supermarket hot cross buns, or the single fancy one he bought from our local sourdough bakery. Mum rolls her eyes – how can we play when there is important work to be done? I shoo him away when he comes to me, too anxious about Mum to be blindfolded. I am already mentally preparing to take her to hospital after the GP visit. With only two weeks to go before I fly to Greece, I won't leave if she is unwell. Perhaps this trip just isn't meant to happen.

When the ingredients are mixed, Mum pushes me aside. The kneading is her job. She scoops the dough away from the sides of a large basin, then presses down on it with her knuckles. She puts her whole body into it.

'Should your mum be doing that?' asks George, serious now. 'What about her heart?'

'I don't think I can do anything to stop her.'

I ring the pharmacist again and get through this time. He confirms that he found an irregular heartbeat. He says it could be his monitor, but it's worth checking out, particularly now that I've told him she's had a stroke. I ring the doctor's surgery. When I describe the problem to the receptionist, she tells me she has an evening appointment available.

It's now after 4 pm. I tell Mum that we're due to see the doctor that evening.

'What about the *koulouria*? They won't be finished by then.' She starts to stumble over her words, gets nervous.

'Dolores and I will finish them. Don't worry.'

The first batch is ready to go in our new oven, but we can't light it. I sit on the floor and stare at the oven dials, fiddling with them. Nothing happens. Is this an omen?

A few minutes later, Dolores presses a button on the display, and it starts.

'Turn it up so we can do them more quickly,' Mum says, all aflutter. Time is running out.

I do as she says. Several minutes later, a burning smell wafts through the kitchen. We've burnt both the bottom row and the top.

I take them out. Perhaps I have put a hex on the *koulouria*. Maybe I'm being punished by a higher power for prioritising a mere mortal over more important spiritual concerns. Perhaps it's just the new oven. I switch the knob over to the fan-forced setting, turn the heat down.

'What a shame,' says Mum.

'We'll have to throw them out,' I say.

'We can't do that.' Mum puts the tray over the sink, asks for a knife, and starts scraping their black tops.

'We have to go, Mum,' I say, turning the oven off, leaving the remaining half-baked koulouria inside, resigned to this batch being a failure too.

On the way to the doctor, my head feels like it's got a tight band around it. For the past few weeks, I've been making daily task lists, powering through the many things I need to do before I leave for Greece. I haven't factored in Mum being unwell. Mentally, I put her health at the top of the list, trumping the now trivial tasks below it. I am reminded again of how insignificant everyday things seem when one's health is in jeopardy.

As we're waiting, I talk to Mum about the need to relax, to try to sleep better.

'How am I going to sleep when you're gone? Do you think I will be able to relax then? Have you really booked your trip?'

'I have, Mum. I know it's not easy. Not for you, or for me. But I'll be okay. I'll ring regularly. Please don't let anything happen to you while I'm gone. I will never forgive myself if you have another stroke for worrying for me!'

'*Pppfft*, I'm not worried about dying. I've lived my life. I worry about you and the family ...'

'We're all going to be fine. George has it covered. And they will visit once a week – you can cook for them.'

She smiles, looks comforted by the idea of doing something useful while I'm gone.

The doctor calls us in. He isn't Mum's regular doctor, and he takes his time to read the test results and letters from the hospital. I convey what the pharmacist said. He takes Mum's blood pressure and listens to her heart carefully.

'I can't hear any irregularities,' he says, and then tells Mum, 'Your heart is surprisingly good for someone your age.'

When I explain what he's said to Mum, she smiles. 'Thank you. You a *very good doctor*.'

On the way out, she says, 'See. I told you it was nothing. I hope the *koulouria* are okay.'

I hope so too.

After I drop Mum off, I realise the tightness around my head is gone. When I get home, I open the oven door cautiously, expecting the worst. I see that the residual heat has cooked the *koulouria* perfectly. I ring Mum, and she is pleased. We will both sleep well tonight.

The next day, I take a walk to our local cemetery where Dad is buried. We moved into the suburb soon after he died. After months of looking at homes on the other side of town, the right home became available in the area. Superstitiously, I felt that Dad had helped us find our home from beyond the grave, perhaps so that I could more regularly light his candle and tend to his grave.

The ritual of lighting the vigil lamp on his tomb is calming; making sure there is oil in the glass, lighting the wick, placing it carefully back into is holder; putting flowers in the vase, lighting the incense and waving it back and forth over the gravesite. Usually I find myself silently talking to Dad, mostly to reassure him that I haven't forgotten him, that I still love him, even if I don't quite come often enough. Today, I silently tell him my news.

I'm finally going to Ikaria, Dad. I know you probably won't approve, because I'm leaving the family. But I do think you'll understand the need to be true to something that feels important. Yes, I'll be safe. Don't worry.

I know my father was proud of me, and that still gives me courage. I touch the top of the gravestone reassuringly, as if Dad can really see me and be comforted by my action.

Now, apart from finalising several work projects over the next two weeks, making sure that the family has everything that they need, and packing myself and my belongings to take an overseas trip, I'm ready to leave.

Arriving

As the plane touches down in Athens I feel a mixture of guilt and elation. Guilt at leaving my family behind in Australia; elation at being in the country where my parents and ancestors were born, where I still have several relatives. As I walk across the tarmac, I am struck by the familiar smell of diesel, one I always associate with my first heady days in downtown Athens some twenty-five years ago now. Being here feels like a homecoming of sorts.

In the terminal, *Theio* Spiro, my father's brother, materialises from behind a column before I've even picked up my luggage. Somehow, he has managed to bypass security. It's been seven years since I last saw him, and he is portlier, greyer, his moustache now reminiscent of my grandfather's. I fear that I might see my father in his features and start crying, but *Theio* is too plump and sunny, where Dad was angular and serious. He is with my first cousin Semina, who hugs me tightly. I get teary, but for different reasons, thinking back to my farewell embraces with George and the kids at the airport in Melbourne.

Theio introduces me to a middle-aged woman, an airport security controller who happens to be his next-door neighbour. I don't need the loudspeaker blaring instructions in Greek on how to claim your baggage in an orderly fashion to know I have arrived in Greece.

In the car, after catching up on how everyone is and what they are doing, we get to the crux of what's important in Greece at this moment. The economy. How difficult things have been. How Greeks are still trying to make the best of an untenable situation. How trade has almost stopped completely. Semina, who works for a multinational telecommunications company, is one of the lucky young people who has a job. In fact, two of the four members of my uncle's family work. This is cause for celebration.

As we drive out of the airport carpark, Semina asks about kangaroos, bushfires, floods. She talks breathlessly, quickly; her long black hair and big brown eyes moving constantly. It's hard for her to get her head around the sheer size of Australia – she is astounded at the idea of it having three time zones.

At home, my aunty Eleni has prepared lunch – baked potatoes, Italian lettuce salad with pomegranate seeds, cheese pie, a few pieces of grilled kabana. *Theio* Spiro opens a bottle of Greek wine, and they ask me more questions about the family. I pull out my phone to show them some photos: the kids, our backyard, the wood-fired oven George has built. A bit of the village in the city. They are impressed.

After a while, I start to fade, and they send me off to bed. Although I have been awake for more than thirty-five hours, I lie there, wired, thinking about how far I am from home. There is a pervasive sense of unreality, and I feel teary again – I am a grown woman, but I feel vulnerable, like a child. I know that sleep will help, but I toss and turn.

I wake a few hours later to my uncle's voice at the door, talking to someone about whether to wake me or leave a note. I get up and he asks me if I'm up for an excursion with the next-door neighbours. It appears his security controller neighbour hasn't eaten since breakfast and has invited them out to eat souvlaki at Mount Lykavitos a little out of Athens. I throw on some clothes, smiling to myself – we are in Greece, and these are the very spontaneous happenings that it is famous for. Despite the financial crisis, some things will never change.

That night, I lie in bed late, tired and overwhelmed by the events of the day, Greek words streaming through my brain, images of shops flying past, groups of people sitting at tables eating. I feel an ache for my family and am suddenly conscious of how far from home I am. How am I going to get through a whole month without my own family?

The next day, the first day of May, I wake early with jetlag, but last night's worries have dissipated. My aunty sends my uncle and I out into the warm morning sunshine to pick flowers for a wreath to put up beside the door. This practice is supposed to bring people closer to nature and to celebrate the 'coming of May' my aunt explains. The month of May was named after the Roman goddess Maia, meaning midwife, nurse and mother in Greek. The tradition has its roots in ancient times, with May dedicated to Demeter, the goddess of agriculture, and her daughter Persephone, who would return to her mother during that month, after spending the winter with Hades in the underworld.

My uncle asks if I'm up to visiting his and my father's sister before lunch. Of course, I say. He doesn't tell my aunt we're coming, choosing instead to surprise her. I ask if we can stop somewhere to pick up some sweets. We pull into the carpark of one of the many bakeries we have passed. It is piled high with rustic loaves of bread, and rows upon rows of sticky baklava, syrupy cakes, biscuits and all manner of sweet delicacies. Despite it being a public holiday, it is open: my uncle says that bakeries are open every day of the year. Clearly, Greeks can't do without their carbs.

Theia Eleni appears on the veranda, looking a little bewildered to see me. She looks older, her face more reminiscent of Dad's, I think with a pang. She kisses both my cheeks, asks after the family, and soon disappears into the kitchen. My cousin George and his son are washing the car across the road. They greet us warmly, then excuse themselves to finish the job.

Theia Eleni comes back with Greek coffee, plates and forks for the cake.

She sits next to me and laments that her husband, Panagioti, my uncle, has passed away since she saw me last.

'He is gone, and I am all alone, Spiridoula.'

'At least you have your sons across the road, your beautiful grandchildren,' I say.

She nods. 'Yes, my grandkids keep me going.'

My cousin Sakis appears from the house he lives in next to his brother. He kisses me and looks at me closely. I wonder what he makes of the changes in my face. I think back to the first time I came to Greece, when we would spill out of nightclubs together in the early morning hours. Or sit on this very same veranda, talking into the night. Twenty-five years have passed since then.

As I eat my cake, I look towards *Theio* Spiro, who is gently advising my cousin about managing their father's estate. I think how naturally he has stepped in to fill the hole now that Panagioti has passed away.

Despite my cousins being middle-aged men, with responsibilities and families of their own, it's comforting to know they still have a father looking out for them, even if he is not their own. No doubt it makes my uncle feel needed, now that he hasn't got paid work to occupy him.

When we return home, my cousin Semina has plans for me. She wants to show me Athens, to make sure I have a good time in the few days I am here.

'You don't want to just hang out with the oldies!' she jokes.

I laugh. I am fifteen years older than her, and some twenty years younger than her parents – midway between her generation and theirs.

We take the underground train into the city, and soon we spill out in the sunshine at Constitution Square. We are hit with a cacophony of sound: tourists, seagulls and vendors who are peddling everything from bread rolls to garish floral head arrangements to celebrate May Day.

We make our way across the square and upstairs to a rooftop bar that looks out to the Acropolis.

Semina and I debate whether it's too early to have a drink, and decide on coffee. She notes that in Greece, drinking is part of enjoying company, eating food, having a good time. It's not an end in itself. She tells me she worked in Silicon Valley for a time.

'My time in the US was good, but it was all about work. You got home at night exhausted, and then you started again the next day. Got drunk on the weekends, ate lots of take out. We had to show our colleagues there was a different way of doing things, made sure they went out during the week, enjoyed the moment, joked and laughed in the office. I work hard here, but at least we have this ...' She waves her hand across the outdoor bar. People, sunshine, life. And the Acropolis.

'Why would you want to give this up?!' I ask.

She laughs. Why indeed?

Later than evening when we get home, I find my uncle sitting with his neighbours on a bench diagonally opposite his house. The bench was built by one of the neighbours. When I asked if he needed a permit from the local council, my uncle scoffs. 'If they want to, they can come and take it away.'

We sit on the bench, and I watch my uncle debrief the day's events with an elderly gent, talk to another neighbour who walks past with her dog. Just as we're about to go in, a teenager and his dad join us, and we stay a little longer. By the time we return to the house, the sun has gone down on this, the first day of spring.

—

The Ancient Greeks said, '*Pan metron ariston*.' Everything in moderation. If you live a life of extremes, you lose balance. Everything is necessary, even problems.'

Theio Spiro and I are having a breakfast of rusks, tahini, honey and black coffee. Like many Greeks, he normally skips breakfast, but is partaking in the ritual to keep me company. As the caffeine takes effect, *Theio* Spiro fires up to the task of telling me what makes for a good life.

'If you expect everything to be pleasant, it just doesn't happen. You can't live without problems, Spiridoula. In Greek, we have a saying: "He who is happy is in his own world." As if he is too stupid to experience life properly. We humans like to be troubled, we're masochists!'

I laugh. Sometimes happiness feels so elusive. The more one strives for it, the further it seems out of reach. *Theio*'s philosophy is much more pragmatic.

'All you can hope to do is solve your problems so that they don't cost you psychologically,' he says. 'And each day, to have some pleasant moments.'

He takes another sip of his coffee. Spreads a second rusk with honey. His wife is not here to berate him about eating too much.

'You know, later tonight, I might have a different philosophy. This is my feeling over coffee this morning!' he continues, laughing in a self-deprecating way, as if to commit to a definitive opinion would cost *him* psychologically.

After breakfast, *Theio* Spiro dons his reading glasses and fires up his little laptop to continue searching for specialty camera shops. He is looking for a charger to suit George's retro-style camera. In the flurry to leave Australia, I'd forgotten to pack it.

It's not the first time he's helped me in the past few days. He's found the right SIM card and best data deal, so I can use my mobile phone in Greece; solved why the wifi connection won't allow me to video call the family; and helped me decipher online bus timetables to prepare for the next leg of my journey to the south of Greece. I think back to my early travels in Greece, when I would write letters back home, and make occasional phone calls from payphones. With the more sophisticated options available to me now, there's no going back, but part of me hankers for the ritual of stepping out and making phone calls from the local square, for the more considered work of laying down ink on paper. Writing the words felt more meaningful than quickly typed obligatory updates on Facebook.

I watch my uncle, glasses perched on the tip of his nose, moustache quivering in concentration. This is a man who grew up in a village without a phone, now earnestly trying to master the vagaries of the internet. It makes me think about my own father, who passed away twelve years ago now. What would he make of me sitting with his brother? I think Dad would be proud that their bond, formed more than half a century ago, has stretched across the seas and over time. It's meant that *Theio* has naturally, and without question, stepped in as father figure for me these past few days I've been in Athens. He and my aunty have fed me, given me a bed to sleep in, and now he's armed me with his take on what makes for a good life.

I feel buoyed. I'm ready to start the next leg of my journey, to visit my *Theia* Kanella and catch up with more cousins.

Connecting

As the bus pushes through and under the mountains, entering the smaller villages of the southern Peloponnese, I feel myself relaxing. I'd forgotten how pretty the white stone houses set back from unsealed roads were, trellised roses and jasmine lining their front yards; the busy village squares, tavernas filled with stooped men playing backgammon. On being flagged by old women laden with shopping, or teens returning from school, the bus driver stops by the road. We whiz past sheds piled high with animal feed and fertiliser.

My cousin Dionysios picks me up from the bus station. His is darkly tanned, unshaven, his movements energetic. His lifts me completely off my feet in a bear hug and talks to me in English. He needs to practise, he says. I laugh and tell him I need to practise my Greek.

I sneak into my aunt's house, and make my way into the kitchen. *Theia* Kanella, dad's sister, comes around the door. She has grown her hair long, and tied it back in a bun like my grandmother used to do. Her face is thinner, and seems much smaller than the last time I was here. She is a little frail – but she looks right somehow, as if this is how an older woman who has been widowed, who has raised kids and grandkids, and who has worked very, very hard, should.

I told myself I wouldn't cry when I saw her, but I can't help it. We sit on the settee in the kitchen, and I hold her hands as she talks. I don't trust myself to speak without sobbing. She composes herself before I can, and she talks while I just sit there. One of her other sons, Stathis, turns up and her eighteen-year-old grandson, Achilleas, eats and watches us, his face unlined, curious, beautiful. He places his plate on the sink, banters with Uncle Stathis about girls, kisses us on the cheek and leaves to go home to study for his exams.

Stathis fusses around us, making coffee, cleaning the already clean bench top. His hair has grown down his back, grey and wavy. 'Spiridoula *mou*,' he calls over his shoulder, 'I am a fifty-year-old bachelor living with his widowed mother in her seventies.' He throws the dish cloth around in mock disgust at the blow that life has dealt him.

'Do not be concerned if you hear us bickering – we fight a hundred times a day.'

I am not concerned about their bickering, as this is what oils Greek households and keeps them healthy.

Stathis sets us up at the table in the garden. He places pillows on the chair for his mother and brings us coffee. We talk about who has died and who is still going since my trip with the family several years ago. I drink the viscous black coffee, blink into the midday sun, find it hard to believe I am here.

Later, *Theia* Kanella shows me her garden, an expanse of vegetable patches she has created from several metres of land that was laying idle. There's not much at this time of year she says – some leeks, onions, silverbeet, peppers and the first of the tomatoes.

She says Stathis was upset with her when she started clearing the space.

'You should have seen what was on this field, rocks, hard dirt, things we had dumped. Stathis was livid that I, with my rheumatoid arthritis and lung problems, was clearing a field. But I said, "Leave this to me. There are some things you simply don't know about." My aunty has grown up on the land; she is an expert at clearing and planting, nurturing and bringing life forth from the earth.

The garden is now at the point where they hardly ever need to go shopping for fresh produce. Along with cutting down on meat, the garden has helped keep their living costs down. My aunt's pension has been cut. Stathis has been out of work for several years, his once thriving business a thing of the past. Dionysios is now living with them on his modest policeman's pension. It's hard.

Stathis has prepared lunch and we go inside to eat. He has a pot of vegetables stuffed with herbs and rice, greens from the garden sautéed with onions, stewed chicken pieces with vegetables, and chicken livers. There is the requisite feta and olives, bread drizzled with olive oil and oregano. We toast with wine and each of us takes what we like; my aunt is fasting, so she avoids the meat and cheese; Dionysios favours the chicken; Stathis and I stick with the vegetable dishes. I tentatively sample the chicken livers, but they are too rich for my taste.

Dionysios knows I am travelling with his ex-wife to Ikaria. I tell him that I feel a little awkward about it. He tells me he's good with it, asks if there is anything I want to know about Ikaria from the time he was stationed there as a policeman. He says he started out in the island's capital Agios Kirikos, then in the small mountain village of Christos Raches. I ask if there was even anything to do there as a policeman.

'Very little. Just the odd altercation between neighbours sometimes. They were good times. The Ikarians were good to us, kept giving us things. Chickens, vegetables, honey …

'But you have to know that they are a strange people. They move to their own rhythms. If you want something in a restaurant, they will get it for you in their own good time. They're not going to run after you. They don't rush, they simply don't care. Don't think that their longevity has got to do with the food, or clean air, or even movement. It's because they don't give a shit ...

'And, if you must know, the women there are in charge. They run everything. And as for their sexuality, let's just say that their morals are a little loose ...'

I'm intrigued by this, but he won't be drawn further. He says I will need to see for myself.

'Anyone who is not of the place, be they from Athens or Australia, are outsiders. They won't trust you, they won't tell you what's what the first time. Maybe the second time you meet them they'll let you in. Or not. You will have a nice holiday, but I don't know if you will learn anything at all.'

Now that I am in Greece, I feel strangely relaxed, with few expectations. In so many ways I have learnt so much from the Ikarians already – the Ikarians I have met on my computer screens, the Ikarians I have read about in research papers, the Ikarians I've watched on television.

In a few short weeks, I will visit their little rugged island and see for myself. But whatever happens, I'm grateful to them. They've helped me rediscover my more gregarious, irreverent self. They've helped me understand that I need to move and eat well and engage with my life most of the time, not just in half-hearted spurts. They've reached across the seas and inspired me to live better. And they've bought me here, to my aunt's generous table.

Over the ensuing days, I spend most of my time with *Theia* Kanella. We fossick in a small, dank outhouse for seeds that she has placed in jars and carefully labelled in handwriting that looks like my father's – *tomato, cucumber, zucchini*. I watch her plant the seedlings, her arthritic hands expertly working the soil. I help her by bringing the hose and seedlings in tiny pots to her side, but it's clear she's in charge. I observe her as she places oregano in trays to dry in the sun, shifting it as the sun moves across the sky.

The day after setting out the oregano, she brings it in and grinds it down through a colander, bottles it neatly, labels it with the date. It joins the many jars of jam she has made over the summer. She shows me a large box of egg noodles she made last year, their earthy smell rising as she exposes them to the air. She checks that they haven't become infested with mites, then seals them up properly before putting the box away.

I marvel at her energy, despite her ailing health.

'I've got to keep going,' she says. 'What can I do? Just sit here and wait to die?'

In the mornings, Stathis checks in on her, listens for her breathing. I sense his fear that her ailing lungs might fail in the night. What if she doesn't wake? When she opens her eyes, he brings her oxygen tank and mask to her.

After breakfast, my aunt lets me brush her hair and plait it before she winds in around in a knot.

'I find it hard to do the bit at the back.'

'I like doing it for you. Your hair reminds me of *Yiayia*'s ...' I say.

'Hers was so much nicer than mine.'

Yiayia's hair was thick and long, always wound neatly into a plaited bun. *Theia* Kanella tells me she washed it once a week in ash that came from the hearth which she mixed with the soap she made herself. The ash kept her hair glossy and thick.

'When she came to live with me, she wanted me to wash it in ash,' says *Theia* Kanella. 'I said to her "Mother, where are we going to find ash here?" It was her one indulgence; she was so proud of her hair.'

I am glad to be able to offer something to my aunt in the short time I am here. There is something very primal, very intimate in brushing her hair, plaiting it for her. She says that this is the one thing that she cannot ask Stathis to do.

Theia Kanella raised her boys alone after her husband died young. She worked hard, mostly doing night shifts as an orderly in a hospital. She's coaxed and cajoled and grown three rowdy boys into men. I watch her with her grandsons, who pop in after school most days, chiding them, berating them if they step out of line, feeding them. She still works hard, despite her ailments. I find myself, a grown woman, deferring to her opinion out of respect for her age, for her experience. She is the undisputed matriarch of the house.

Dionysios takes my aunt and I to visit my grandparent's village where Kanella, Spiro and my father grew up. I brace myself to see the old family home. Last time I was here, I was upset to see it in near ruins, the roof looking ready to collapse, the back porch and door already caved in. Since then, *Theio* Spiro has sold it to a fellow villager on the proviso that he rebuilds it in the same traditional style. The house now stands solid; its rustic sandstone walls decorated with shuttered windows, the back porch finished elegantly in marble. I feel happy to see it revived in this way.

In the small cemetery where my grandparents are buried, I'm taken aback to see a photo of my father on my grandparents' grave. I hold back a little while my aunt lights a candle beside the grave, composing myself. We make our way into the church, fill one of the vigil lamps with oil and light the wick. There is something comforting in undertaking these small rituals, remembering and honouring those who have gone before us.

On another day we drive to my uncle Panagioti's village and light the candle by his grave too. It's surreal to see his photo on the headstone; last time I was here, he was alive. I feel grateful that he was well until a few days before his death; hunting boars, tending his hives, drinking coffee at the local cafeneion.

My visit is all too short, and on my last day there, I sit on *Theia* Kanella's bed while she takes in her oxygen. I pass over her steroids. From this vantage point, I can see the ravages that time has left on her; lines deeply etched in her cheeks, the tendons and lax muscles around her neck protruding under thin skin. Her eyes are teary. We don't speak. We both know this is probably the last time we will see each other.

Philosophising

My cousin Dionysios drives me to the town of Kalamata to reunite with my first cousin Natassa, from Mum's side of the family. We arrive to find Natassa dragging a trolley up the stairwell to her apartment, filled with food from the *laiki*, the local market. I introduce her to Dionysios, and she quickly puts the trolley to one side and takes us up to the formal parlour and serves us drinks. She waves away the grandeur, a bit embarrassed, 'These things belonged to my husband's family. He likes them ...'

After Dionysios leaves, Natassa tells me we're going to stay in their *exoteriko* (summer home), which is in the hills some thirty minutes out of Kalamata. When her husband, Sotiris, arrives, he greets me warmly, and then we get down to the business of trying to fit everything into their small car. There is food, four overnight bags, the dog and their twelve-year-old daughter, Olga. Somehow, we manage.

After only one day together, Natassa and I have returned to the relationship we had when we visited as a family when I was seven – Natassa is the leader and I am the follower. I accompany her to the beach, water her garden, spring clean her kitchen, and convince her daughter to go to bed.

This morning, Natassa has decided on string beans for lunch. Now, after topping and tailing the beans, she is lying on a garden chair that's seen better days, smoking. A few years older than me, she is wearing her oldest garden clothes, her hair unkempt. Her breasts are spilling out of her top, a sliver of her bra lace showing. There are no formalities here.

'Why are you going to Ikaria?' she asks, as we look down on the *terrazas* below us and the sea a few hundred metres away.

'To see what it takes to live longer. And better,' I reply.

'I'll tell you what it takes to live longer. You need to have lots of sex,' she says and laughs raucously.

'I don't mean just the *praxis* (the act),' she continues. 'I'm talking about *eros*, sex with feeling, with *intimacy*.

'Also, you can't have bad feelings towards others. Keep jealousy away from your heart.'

She sinks down further into the chair, feet up, pulling at her cigarette, ash falling to the ground. She is just getting started, clearly enjoying herself. 'I don't think it's the food we eat that brings sickness, it's about our psychology. It's not just about diet – *ppphh*, that's nothing – it's about angst, and how we can avoid it.

'You need to have dreams, to be able to step away from your life and see if from afar – not microscopically, not myopically. And don't put too much pressure on yourself.'

I love the Greek language; even when crudely expressed, it is the language of poetry, of the soul. As Natassa lets loose, I'm reminded of Cavafy's poem 'Ithaca':

> *Laistrygonians and Cyclops*
> *angry Poseidon – don't be afraid of them:*
> *you'll never find things like that on your way*
> *as long as you keep your thoughts raised high,*
> *as long as a rare excitement*
> *stirs your spirit and your body.*

'Are you listening?' asks Natassa. 'The most important thing is to give of yourself. When you give love, you get love back, and that fills you up. Don't infect your heart and your soul with bad feeling.' She looks at me like a stern school teacher who expects her recalcitrant student to hold onto her every word.

'Natassa, these are all good things, but you told me yourself you are tired. You are exhausted actually.' I look pointedly at the full ashtray before her and raise an eyebrow.

'Well, it's clear that I don't follow my own advice! In my work, I try and give what I want to get back. But in my life overall, I don't do these things.' She draws on her cigarette.

'All I want is to grow my flowers, to share things with others, to give something away, to have a meal with those I love. That's what gives me pleasure.'

Sotiris comes up to the *terraza* and joins the conversation. He too agrees that giving is what counts. He recounts visiting nearby villages around Kalamata when he first started out in the family business as an oil trader.

'The villagers looked forward to seeing us. We were their bosses in a way, we paid them money for their oil. They didn't use banks then. The money they got from us was their income for the year.

'One thing I found is that the poorest people were the most generous,' he continues. 'Even if they didn't have anything to eat, they set the table for you, gave you bread, and *horta* and cheese, whatever they had from their farm. They fed you, then they cleared the table. Played music. Danced. They trusted you with their oil, didn't question the price, let you have the dregs for free. These were content people. They didn't have much, but they appreciated what they had.

'The rich people, they didn't even offer you a coffee, though we were there for several hours, collecting their many litres of oil. They negotiated everything to the last drachma. And they seemed unhappy. Deeply unhappy.

'The trick is not to have more money than you need, but to have your health. Without your health, you are nothing. And to be content with what you have at any given moment. Money is nothing if you are not content.'

I think back to the documentary I watched about the Ikarians, about being content with enough. I look around me on the terraza; the string beans in a bowl, a plate of cumquats, conversation that ebbs and flows. At this moment, I feel content.

—

Sotiris's sister Clare and her husband George have invited us and a group of their friends to Sunday lunch. We are sitting at an outdoor table set near a vegetable garden and olive grove. I'm in the company of a microbiologist, a surgeon, a few mechanical engineers and a poet. We've just finished feasting on roast lamb, livers wrapped in entrails, pork cutlets and sausages, all cooked on an outdoor spit. These were accompanied by baked potatoes and several salads, dips and bread. The meat has come from local farms, the salad vegetables from the garden. Though we have finished eating, the table is still groaning with leftover food.

After I introduced myself to the group, they embraced me and my Ikarian quest with gusto. Everyone is keen to contribute their thoughts on what factors help us to live a long time. But, as always, the conversation veers from that to what it takes to live well. To be healthy. To live a meaningful life. I've tapped into something that concerns us all. And here in Greece, everyone is an expert. The art of dialogue and argument is still alive and well, with anything and everything up for discussion. And it's usually explored loudly, passionately.

'Are you meaning to tell me that Socrates wasn't stressed? Stress, productive stress, has always been around. It's necessary for creativity, for progress,' says one of the guests.

'Like hell he was stressed. Stress is a modern creation, something that we don't need. That, and that alone, is the reason the Ikarians live such a long time. They simply don't get stressed,' says another.

'Look, to work hard, to worry about your family, to get ahead – this is not stress, this is life. You can't just sit to the side of your life, observing it. You need to live it, be in the thick of it. And yes, inevitably this causes stress,' counters Maria, the microbiologist.

'It's when you don't *release* stress that it turns to illness,' she continues, on a roll now. 'The old ones, our elders, they used to say that if you don't express yourself, if you don't release what is inside you, it will become an ulcer. It's well known now that psychological pain can cause physical pain ...'

'Do you know what the actual word "*anthropos*" (a human), means?' Maria asks me.

I admit I don't know.

'*Anathron ol apope.* This translates from ancient Greek as "to critique everything you see". To be human is to explore, to ask questions, to hold your head up, to *engage*. In its essence, it is not the absence of stress.'

Dessert arrives, an orange and almond jelly that Clare has made from the oranges in her grove, and frozen strawberry ice-cream George has made. The orange desert is intense, tangy; the ice-cream creamy and fresh. George talks at length about how he had to stir the milk with a fork. While I don't understand every word everyone is saying, I know enough to be aware that the conversation has become lewd as they talk about how much whipping is required, how hard one needs to do it, whether one has a good enough tool.

Dessert is followed by homemade *limoncino*, and then a sour cherry liqueur, an offering from a guest who made a batch last year. The conversation veers towards the food, and Clare shares her recipes. We in turn salute her for her hospitality. She hardly sits down, pours drinks, offers food constantly. The music is turned up, and someone gets up to dance.

We chink glasses and drink to life. The conversation gets even more raucous. The poet asks me why the tax office won't allow him to declare his profession as a poet – isn't that as legitimate as being a mechanical engineer? His eyes dance, challenging me across the table. He gets up and recites a ditty about a widow in Gucci glasses and push-up bra, replete with hand gestures. There is much laughter.

I marvel once again at the elegance of the Greek language when it comes to social connection – it's like observing a passionate dance between lovers, the words lilting and swaying around each other in ever more joyful circles.

George sidles up to me and asks if I have heard of Stamatis Moraitis.

'Yes, he's the one who got my started on this journey,' I say, excited. 'I read his story in the *New York Times*. He reminded me of my grandparents, of my uncle Panagiotis, perhaps a little of my father. He's the reason why I'm here.'

'I have a friend who's from Ikaria, who knew him,' says George, then tells the story about how when Stamatis moved from the US to Ikaria, he had cancer and was frail and sick. He also tells me how, after forty years, Stamatis was still drawing a pension from America, even though he should have been dead a long time ago. The US authorities got suspicious, and sent auditors to look into it. They were amazed that he was still alive, still entitled to his pension. He'd even outlived the doctors who diagnosed him.'

'I heard that he died only a few years ago,' I say.

'Yes, they say he was more than a hundred years old.'

'I'm going to find his grave and light a candle for him, to

thank him for starting me off on this little quest of mine.' I look George in the eyes. 'Thank you so much for your generous table.'

'It's nothing. I can tell you're a good person. At the end of the day, that's all that counts. And this –' he says, extending his arm around the table. 'Being with friends, eating good food, talking. It's a good way to pass the time now that we have retired.'

We chink glasses. I agree. It's a great way to pass the time, even for those of us who haven't yet retired. An island song comes on and he grabs my hand to dance.

—

My final visit to relatives before I head off to Ikaria is to my mother's niece, Smaragthi, in the town of Kalamata. Soon after my arrival, Smaragthi takes me off to spend a day at the beach in her mother's village, some twenty kilometres from Kalamata. The village is set on loamy earth, where my aunty spent most of her adult life growing oranges, tomatoes, cantaloupes and watermelon.

Since I was last here seven years ago, two international resorts have been built on the seashore. The gleaming buildings with their manicured lawns look incongruous among the rustic village homes and small farm holdings. At the beach, we sit on sun chairs, waiting for someone to take our coffee order. When Smaragthi realises no one is coming, she goes up to the hotel while I watch English tourists take wind surfing and canoeing lessons. Smaragthi stomps back across the boardwalk twenty minutes later, two cold coffees in hand.

'They wouldn't let me buy coffee because we didn't have a room number,' she fumes. 'I had an argument with the wait staff. I said I've been coming to this beach all my life. The beach is free. They gave me my coffee.'

The last time I was here, we had taken my aunty with us, sat on the sand, eaten one of her oranges. Now my aunty has passed away. We only just visited her grave, placed flowers and lit a candle. I'd taken photos to show Mum. Smaragthi talks about how much she misses her mother. I think how lucky I am to still have mine. Since her stroke I am seeing her much more and I ring her daily. I appreciate her more now than I ever have before.

After we get back from the beach I ring Mum and tell her about what a wonderful time I'm having seeing relatives, and update her on everyone's news. Then I listen to Smaragthi talk with Mum on the phone, lovingly, reassuringly.

'Now, I plan to visit you early next year, so promise me you won't get sick before then. Spiridoula is well, we are looking after her. We'll send her home safe and sound, don't worry. I just want you to look after yourself!'

I sit nearby, crying, touched by Smaragthi's words. Though she hasn't seen my mother since she was a child, she speaks to her as if she were her own.

Afterwards we Skype with George and the kids. Dolores is cooking a chicken and chickpea curry, Emmanuel is doing his homework. George tells me proudly that tonight he is on top of the washing, he's vacuumed and mopped the floor, and that everyone seems to be coping in my absence.

'We miss you. I think we thought a month would fly, but it's going very slowly.'

'I miss you too.'

I've only been eight days in Greece, but it feels like more, as if I've been travelling for months. Immersing myself in other people's lives has helped me see my own life more clearly. While I'm enjoying being surrounded by my Greek family, it's reassuring to know that I will return home at the end of the month.

In the meantime, George and I keep sending each other

snapshots from our day – he sends me a picture of the olive tree in our autumn garden; I, of the clothes drying on a rack on Smaragthi's veranda, Kalamata's rooftops in the background; he, an image of my mother serving the children a huge tray of *pasticcio*, a baked pasta and meat dish.

Today, I am glad that we're staying home, glad to give Smaragthi a massage to alleviate the pain she's suffering from a migraine. It's the least I can do to thank her for her hospitality.

Smaragthi texts her adult children to tell them not to call, switches her phone off and sets soft music playing on the computer in the next room.

'We'll use balsam oil,' she says.

'What's that?' I ask.

'Your mum would know it. They used it on the soldiers in the war. It was good for healing wounds.'

She places a cup of the resin-like oil beside the bed, it's dark-pink hue luminous under the lamp light.

'You're my guest, I should have taken you to the beach, not have you give me a massage ...'

'It's okay. I'd like to,' I say. 'Anyway, we went to the beach yesterday.'

'Still, you came all the way from Australia ...'

Despite her words, Smaragthi lies down in expectation. I laugh. This is something my mother, her beloved aunty, would do. As I try and ease her migraine away with long smooth strokes, I think how good it feels to give something of myself to make someone feel good.

—

A few days later, the time has finally come for my trip to Ikaria and I'm very excited. I am back at the Athens airport, this time to board a flight to the island. When I see Ikaria up on the digital screen at the terminal, along with a gate number, I feel a surge of excitement, snap a picture to share with family and friends. There's no going back now.

With a bit of time to spare, I wander into the airport book-shop. There is an eclectic selection of Greek-themed English language books: Homer, Durrell, Dessaix. My eye surveys the tomes. As is my childhood habit, I wait for a book to 'choose' me, to give me what I need now.

I pick up Lawrence Durrell's *Greek Islands*, first published in the late '70s. Flicking to the index, I find there is a small refer-ence to Ikaria. I turn to the page, and discover that Durrell visited the island on the way to the nearby island of Samos. He writes, 'Unrewarding and rugged Icaria … has an unkempt air, as if it has never been loved by any of its inhabitants.' He goes on to say that it's as if the road system has been 'thought up by a drunken postman'. I close the book quickly and put it back on the shelf. This is not what I need now.

I spy a collection of Greek poets, Seferis and Cavafy among them. I choose Cavafy, who served me well on my travels to Ithaka several years back. Perhaps he will guide me in Ikaria too.

But Durrell has tapped into a deeper fear. What if, after more than two years of waiting to visit Ikaria, I will be disappointed? I take the idea one fanciful step further: what if Ikaria doesn't even really exist, like it's mythical namesake, but is a figment of my overactive imagination?

On the plane, I leaf through the in-flight magazine, play with my phone and eat the *pasteli* (honey sesame bar) they serve, which surprises me with it spicy aftertaste.

After I've been on the plane for a while, I realise I might have a real live Ikarian woman sitting next to me. I make eye contact with her and say, 'The *pasteli* is nice. It's different. I wonder what the spice is?' It's an awkward question, but it's a start.

'Yes, I had it last time I flew.' She reads the back of the packet. 'I'm not sure what it is.'

'Are you from Ikaria?' I ask.

'No, I work there.'

I find out that she is doing her internship at the hospital, a requirement before she specialises to become a doctor. We talk a little about what she wants to specialise in, and what the job opportunities for doctors are in Greece. She tells me there is a list of doctors waiting to be placed, and her name will be added to it. It will likely be several years before she gets a job, on top of the nine years it has taken her to qualify.

She tells me she is thinking about moving to Sweden to work, but she's concerned about being so far from family. She says she is still debating it. I sense her dilemma – the push and pull of wanting a career, and financial security – and the need to be close to family and home. As we discuss her problem, I think about my parents and their own migration journey from Greece to Australia. I don't envy the decision she must make.

I ask if she sees many elderly people at the hospital. She smiles – they are her main clientele. She tells me that the oldest people she sees have the least serious ailments. Generally, they are issues you'd naturally expect to see with ageing, like arthritis.

'The really elderly aren't the ones with the most serious problems – it's those under sixty-five.'

I turn back to my *pasteli*, and ponder how much I have already learnt from Ikaria, though I haven't yet touched down on her shores. In the next two weeks, I wonder what more I will learn from the island where people 'forget to die'.

Landing

As the plane approaches Ikaria, I look down to see jagged craggy cliffs against an impossibly blue sea. I snap a photo for my children through the window.

At the airport I am greeted by a statue of Icarus, his wings and arms stretched out as if about to take off. I can't help but think that I too am about to embark on yet another adventure. I have arrived on this ancient island and I can't stop smiling, even though there is no one yet to which I can direct my joy.

I pick up my luggage and introduce myself to Urania behind the airport's only kiosk. Via email a few weeks back, she kindly agreed to give me a free informal tour of the island, changing her plans to accommodate me – I'd acquiesced, on the proviso that she would let me buy her lunch.

From the airport, we take a short drive to the nearby village of Faro. The road to the town is winding, the cliffs leading down to the sea spectacular, juxtaposed against a stony landscape. I am silent, hardly daring to breathe for fear that this may yet be a dream. But the rocks and sea and sky are so vivid. I really am here.

Faro has several fish tavernas, a few rooms for rent, and an expanse of beach. We step into the leafy courtyard of Evon's café, and Urania introduces me to the owner. When I remark on his Australian accent, Evon tells me he spent quite a bit of his young life in Adelaide.

'Evon is an activist,' Urania tells me, going on to explain that he organises volunteers to clear the beach and to help open old paths like the ones his grandparents used to walk. He's also introduced recycling bins, waste bags for collecting dog faeces and ashtrays at the beach. She notes that change is not always easy and he often comes to loggerheads with the local establishment.

Evon looks quite pleased when Urania says this as he takes our orders. His expression suggests that there's nothing like a bit of conflict to keep you on your toes.

I tell Evon I've come to Ikaria because I'm interested in what makes the elders of the island live so long.

He doesn't hesitate. 'The secret is to work out how to be happy with not too much. Don't stress. Do things slowly.'

Petra and Martin, a German couple Urania spoke to at the airport, join us. I learn they have been coming to the island for many years, like many repeat tourists who visit Ikaria. Urania introduces them to Evon and they discuss how they can support his work. They talk about organising volunteers to clear paths and providing funds to help the process. Urania speaks to Petra and Martin in German, turns to me in a mix of English and Greek, then fires off quick Greek to Evon. My head is reeling with the sound of different languages.

As the conversation ebbs and flows, I ask Urania to tell me a little more about herself. She says she originally studied economics, with a view to helping run the family tour business. When I say I can't imagine her as an economist, she rolls her eyes and admits she mostly did it to please her father. But she always wanted to study art. She goes on to say that in her forties she managed to put herself through a fine art correspondence course with the University of Minnesota. Now she runs the tour business in the summer, paints in the winter. When I ask if she exhibits, she mumbles that her work has been shown in Athens, that there have been a few international exhibitions. She steers the conversation away from herself, back to the island.

After a while, Urania's brother Dimitris arrives with his partner Simone. A fair, fit-looking woman, Simone is from Berlin, where she worked as an actress and dancer, but now teaches yoga and mindfulness on the island. She takes the concept of being happy with very little to a whole new level, explaining that she is working on a project called 'The Big Nothing'. It's about having more faith in the intuitive, organic side of our lives, and connecting our heads and our hearts with the earth as if there is a string between them. We talk about how Western societies are often head-driven, lurching into work and making money and trying to be successful in a linear, more masculine sense.

Our salads arrive, large bowls of rustic lettuce leaves, wedges of tomatoes, thick green olives and pieces of *Kathoura*, a local goat's cheese. More people join us at the table and the conversation bubbles back and forth; there's gossip about a new taverna that has opened up, talk about how the tourist season is likely to pan out this year and what Urania is likely to cook for dinner.

As we're eating, Thodoris, Urania's partner, pulls up in a newly purchased tourist bus. He is a quiet, bearded man, contrasting to Urania's garrulous energy. He takes a seat at the table, orders a burger. He's been up early, driving the school bus, doing the run from one side of the island to the other, and is keen to go home and have a nap. I realise with a start that we've been at the café for a few hours already.

We make our way out to the street and admire the new bus. Evon's Mum needs a lift to the neighbouring town. We all climb on board.

Urania slaps me on the back. 'You're our first guest for the season – I hope you bring us good luck.'

'I hope so too,' I say as I drop a few coins into a little compartment near the front seat. Making a monetary gift when someone makes a large purchase such as a car is an old Greek tradition, a way of wishing them luck. Urania looks at me with surprise, as if I've passed a test. Then she pokes at the coins and jokes that they will help pay for dinner.

Thodoris suggests we stop in the main port town, Agios Kirikos, so I might see the mineral springs, and then wind across the southern side of the island and through the mountains, cutting across to the northern part of the island. This will give me a good sense of the rocky coast and the forested interior, as well as give the new bus a good test run.

'Will you be okay with the steering on the mountain roads?' Urania asks.

'We'll soon see.' Thodoris closes the door, smiling wolfishly.

I wonder what I've got myself in for.

—

As the roads wind along the jagged, rocky coastline, I listen to Urania speaking, though my eyes are drawn ever-downward towards the sea, its majesty contrasting to the dark backdrop of the land. I mentally pinch myself – I'm here on this tiny island in the Mediterranean.

At Agios Kirikos, we walk behind the port, where a small group of people are soaking in the warm springs cut into the rock face. Across the port, we can see the Fourni islands, where Urania is originally from. She tells me that the islands are noted for their mazes of rocks and secret passages, which were once a perfect hideaway for pirates, then jokes that her family is likely to be from pirate stock.

She reminisces about cooking with her mother and other women in the village, gossiping about everything and everyone.

With so many of their menfolk working as fishermen and sailors, the women worked the land, ran the family home, got an education. Urania proudly says that the Greeks on Ikaria, both male and female, are some of the most well educated in the country.

After leaving Agios Kirikos we make our way across the southern side of the island, where we then veer to the right and cut across the mountains. The landscape changes suddenly, and we are in forests of pine and oak. Thodoris is a picture of concentration as he navigates the unfamiliar steering on the bus.

Meanwhile Urania is noting important culinary landmarks: where to get the best *loukoumathes* (honey donuts), where to get the most delicious souvlaki, which establishment makes the most traditional Ikarian food …

She points to a dark stone in the sea, says that it represents the tears of Daedalus, the father of Icarus, when Icarus fell into the sea. The white cliffs behind it represent his grief; the stone changing colour when he lost his son.

Just as the sun starts to come down, we stop at the second, smaller port town of Evdilos on the northern coast of the island, where Urania shows me around the stately captains' houses lining the port.

She points out a plaque of Aristides Foutridis, a resident of the town, and tells me he was the first translator of Cavafy's poems.

'Have you heard of Cavafy?' she asks.

I pull out the small book of his poetry I bought at the airport, telling her that I used his famous poem 'Ithaca' to frame a memoir I wrote some years ago. I explain how this poem has come up at important intervals in my life, reminding me of the importance of honouring the journey, not the destination. Urania's eyebrows rise in surprise as I talk, and I sense something shift between us: I am no longer a tourist, but a friend. We understand each other.

As we walk around Evdilos, Urania talks about her own advocacy work to improve the island. She points out a disused space where the town might build a playground; a wall that could be beautified with some artwork. She talks about the need for progress and more sustainable tourism, while preserving the natural landscape and its wonderful traditions. Already, with more commercial harvesting of the herbs on the island, the beekeepers have complained that their bees didn't produce the toffee-like white heather *reiki* variety last year. She says that the old people knew how to care for the land, taking only what they needed.

'You love this place, don't you?' I say.

'Oh yes!' she replies enthusiastically.

Back on the bus, I tell Urania about how I'd like to talk with some of the elders on the island, and seek her advice on the best way to do this. She sighs a little, as if I am yet one more in a long line of people wanting to talk to elders, mining them for their secrets.

'Recently, I had a journalist here, one of the many who fly in, take their interviews and photos and leave again,' she says. 'I said to him I would organise an interview with a family friend, a widow, but he wasn't to ask her how old she was, what she ate as a child or what the secret to a long life was. He had to agree to let me lead the discussion.

'At her home we sat with her, and I held her hand. I asked her if she could go back to one moment in her life, what it would be? She said it would be to feel the touch of her husband's hand in hers on their wedding day. A tear rolled down her cheek.'

'It was the most poignant moment, Spiri. It led to so many stories and memories of the important things in her life. After everything is gone, life gets distilled into key moments. It's these moments that frame our lives, that give us meaning.

'You can't just barrel in. These are real people, with real lives. You're going to have to find your own way in. It might take time.' She shrugs. She can't help me here.

I feel a little abashed: I'm no different to the other writers in my motivations. But everything Urania says makes sense. I realise I'm going to have to proceed with my plans differently. Be patient. Have faith that I will learn things from the island and its people gradually. And with any luck, I might be able to give something back.

The roads are dark by the time Thodoris pulls up at Thea's Inn. I look at my phone. It's ten o'clock. Where have the nine hours since I arrived gone?

Urania jokes that I have officially become acculturated to Ikarian time. She promises that we will catch up soon, and that I am to ring her if I need anything. We kiss each other on the cheek. I shake Thodoris's hand, thank him for forfeiting his afternoon nap so that I should see the island.

Inside, the taverna is lively. I meet Thea, a tall woman with a shock of curly hair and expressive brown eyes.

'*Koukla*, my doll, you've arrived. Welcome!' she says in a strong American accent.

She introduces me to her husband, Ilias, who runs the family farm and supplies their restaurant. An older man with a generous moustache puts his arm around me, jokes that *he* will take me up to my room. There is laughter all around. I feel nervous until I see that they are joking. I join in, and so my first day in Ikaria comes to an end.

Drinking

I wake to the sound of goats. From the balcony outside my room, I can see the three culprits who woke me, nimbly stepping over rocks and wild greenery to find their breakfast. The craggy rocks lead down to the sea, which is calm on this still morning. It's a luxurious novelty to get up at any time I like, to know my breakfast will be laid out for me.

Before I head downstairs, I try to video call my family, but I can't get through. I feel a pang of anxiety. I've been unable to contact them since arriving on the island.

As I step out into the bright morning light, I see that the town of Nas is little more than a handful of tavernas with a few rooms for rent. I also see why my video call wasn't working; there are roadworks just outside the apartment and the electricity is down. I spot Ilias helping fix the lines, as is a gent who must be in his early nineties – while the older man is not digging himself, he appears to be giving advice to the workmen.

At the Inn, I take a seat in the sun, as close as I can to a view of the sea. There's a long table of young people having breakfast, their voices carrying over to the few of us who are sitting at smaller tables nearby. Thea is playing mother to the group, asking, *Did you all sleep well? Who would like eggs? Have you had enough to eat?*

I order Greek coffee, yoghurt and honey from the waiter. While I'm waiting, I catch the eye of another patron, and we introduce ourselves. Gayle is from Minnesota, and is a long-time friend of Thea's. She comes and stays with her every few years. She tells me that the young people at the neighbouring table are hospitality students on exchange from Kentucky in the US. I laugh and say Ikaria is no doubt a great place to learn how to be hospitable.

As we talk more, Gayle tells me that she is planning to head up to Christos Raches, an inland mountain village, to buy some produce from the women's cooperative there. She's happy for me to join her, and we agree to meet later that morning at a neighbouring town a few kilometres away. I need the exercise after weeks of being chauffeured around.

The walk is a feast for the eyes, as terraced fields and rocky hills plunge deeply down into the sea. Wild poppy flowers grow from unforgiving rock faces and whitewashed homes cascade down the hillside. I take photo after photo with George's camera, though I didn't really have time to learn to use it before I left. I wish he was here to take the photos, to do this beautiful setting justice. As if to emphasise my incompetence, I drop the lens cap several times.

Soon, I reach the scenic village of Armenistis and come across a whitewashed blue and white church tucked away off a quiet road. Above its doorway is a mural of Saint Nicholas, the patron saint of sailors and travellers. I stop to take a photo, dropping the lens cap again, this time into a little enclosed yard a few metres below the road. I wind my way down a narrow path, unlatch a gate, and claim it from its dusty resting place. I tell myself that I must be careful, that no one will be able to find me if I fall in this isolated enclave. As I turn to make my way back to the path, I lose my footing and slip down the ledge, smashing my back against its concrete edge. I'm immobilised by a sharp searing pain, unable to breathe.

I look up to the church and momentarily blame the saint for not protecting *this* traveller. But the saint's gaze remains unchanged in the morning sunshine. I need to look to myself. It's as if, by sheer force of will, I have turned my fear of getting hurt into reality. I slide myself up to sit on the ledge and breathe in slowly. The pain is intense. What if I've fractured a disc, or ruptured a kidney? I'm all alone here. I don't dare get up yet. I reach slowly into my backpack, and pull out my phone to ring my mother.

The familiarity of Mum's voice brings me back to my senses. I describe the church in front of me, the beauty of the island, being woken by goats. She sounds worried and tells me she misses me, that she prays for the day when I get home safely. She assures me that the kids are well taken care off; George is doing a great job. She has been delivering *pasticcio* regularly to our home. George and the kids have been coming once a week to eat at hers. I know she thinks that if they are fed, all will be well. Like me, she shows her love through food.

Talking to Mum helps distract me from the pain and I don't tell her about my fall. When I hang up, I push myself up, inch by inch, and slowly shuffle to the café where I am meeting Gayle, each step resounding painfully into my back. It's late morning, and the café owner is still setting up. He takes me through the menu; recommends the goat's milk ice-cream with mountain herbs. Apparently, the goats outnumber the locals by four to one; goat's milk is definitely on my 'to try' list. The owner comes back with the ice-cream, and a large book, simply titled *Icaria,* by Yiorgos Depolas.

'I hope you have a good time on our beautiful island,' he says after I thank him.

As I wait for Gayle, I flick through the book and am surprised to find that Mikis Theodorakis, one of Greece's most famous composers, was interned on the island in the late 1940s for his leftist sympathies. Theodorakis reflects, 'My years in Icaria were full, heavy and intense and have been forever engraved in my mind.' He writes of the beauty of the island and the warmth of the locals who risked their lives to be generous to the several thousand communist and leftist supporters who were interned here during this time. The islanders helped them to survive in harsh conditions, despite themselves being so poor. The interns, many of whom were well educated, helped build roads, taught locals foreign languages and gave free medical help.

Gayle soon arrives, and I convince her to have the ice-cream; it's good. As I order a serve for her, she admires my ability to speak Greek, lamenting that she must rely on others to translate for her while on the island. She wishes she'd learnt more in her years of coming here. It's at times like these that I'm glad my parents made me learn the language.

As we chat more, Gayle tells me that Thea and the island remind her about what is important in life. They help her 'fill her cup' and take stock after the stresses of city life. She runs a busy health club back home; while she helps others take care of themselves, she herself works very hard to manage it. Now in her fifties, it's come to a point in her life where she needs to sell up, let it go. Her time in Ikaria is always a welcome escape.

We make our way inland towards the village of Christos Raches, up winding mountain roads where we pass terraced ledges, oak and pine forests, a cemetery on a hill in the distance and rows upon rows of olive trees.

Christos Raches centres around a small square with traditional stone buildings and wooden tables. Young children zigzag around the adults, their laughter ringing out.

At the women's cooperative, a little shop that specialises in local produce, I'm delighted to find wild bulbs steeped in vinegar, which were one of my father's favourite foods. The tang of the vinegar tempers their earthy bitterness. I try delicacies that it would be hard to find in Australia: prickly pear jam, rose petal 'spoon' desert and seven-herb liquor. Gayle buys several jams and a few bottles of berry-infused homemade liquors. We stop to have one of the cakes, talking about our lives back home, about Gayle's many trips to the island.

Gayle tells me that her next stop is Afianes Winery, where she is meeting Thea and the hospitality students. She says I'm welcome to come. This is Ikaria after all.

—

The winery is a few kilometres away, nestled in the tiny village of Profitis Elias. As we pull up, we are greeted by a young woman called Nicole, who tells us she runs the winery with her partner, Constantinos, who waves as he walks past, busy setting up for the students.

Nicole brings us books and brochures about the winery, pointing out the prizes it has won. She offers us one of their award-winning desert wines, Tama, telling us it's made from the Fokiano variety of grapes, a special variety grown locally. It's smooth, sweet, decadently fruity.

Gayle asks Nicole how she came to be here. She tells us she is originally from Nafplio in southern Greece, where her parents grew oranges.

She smiles wryly and says, 'I fell in love with my boyfriend, the place and the vines – in a way that I didn't fall in love with my parents' orange groves! It was good for me psychologically.' She shrugs, as if to laugh at her younger, more confused self.

As I take the last sip of the Tama, I joke with Gayle that *this* is probably the secret to why the islanders live such a long time.

The students arrive, and Constantinos shows us around the winery: the huge vat where grapes are pressed by foot; smaller clay vats dug into the ground, where the wine is steeped using methods employed for centuries. Nicole then shows us her favourite item in the one-room folk museum, the *kerastari*, which is a large communal terracotta cup with several spouts, designed to share wine. It's also the name of the communal space set at the back of the winery.

We make our way to a little amphitheatre at the foot of a low hill, and Constantinos regales us with stories of the history of wine making, ranging from the mythic to the modern.

'Now it all started with Dionysios, the god of celebration, wine and orgies ...' The students titter, right on cue. 'While we like to claim Dionysios was born in Ikaria, I have to admit to you that there are a few other places in Greece who also claim him.'

From what I've read of Dionysus, he was the protector of those who did not belong to conventional society. He symbolises the chaotic, the dangerous, the unexpected; represents ritual madness and fertility. I can imagine him having a great time on Ikaria.

'*Pramnios oinos*, or Pramnian wine, was mentioned in Homer's "Iliad",' Constantinos continues. 'His warriors drank a beverage made from wine, goat's cheese, barley flour and herbs. They believed that this drink would make them strong and battle-ready.'

I remember Urania saying yesterday that she has collected a similar recipe from elders in her family and marvel at how some traditions might be passed on, century after century.

'This was not the first time wine was considered a healer – even Hippocrates used it as medicine. He cautioned that it should be drunk in moderation, and mixed with water. Many Ikarians still drink it with water today.

'It is thought that the word "Pramnios"' comes from the Ikarian mountain, Pramnos, where a specific Fokiano grape variety is cultivated. This is one we have tried to create as closely as those made in antiquity.'

Constantinos serves us the same amber-coloured Tama wine we had earlier, and I can feel my head start to get light. The afternoon sun is bearing down.

'At this winery, we are experimenting with technology and tradition. I'm not interested in making big money, I'm interested in extending the palate and doing innovative things. Most of the wines here are in very small production. If you like them, you like them; if you don't, you don't.' He shrugs, laughing.

The second wine we taste is a Begleri, which is cloudy, golden, and much richer that the lighter Australian whites my palate is used to.

'I'm thinking about experimenting with biodynamic processes — all that that crazy shit about using the moon and the planets to guide growing and harvesting!' says Constantinos, smiling almost apologetically.

It doesn't seem so strange to me. I remember my mother telling me they used the very same processes to grow food in her village.

I feel a growing admiration for this amusing young man and his girlfriend, who are taking their family traditions and creating something new from them. It is a little like what I am trying to do with my own family traditions, moulding what my parents and grandparents have taught me into something that fits with my life right now.

The final wine we're offered is simply titled 'Icarus Black'. It's a deep purplish red colour. In the first sip, I can taste the minerals in it. There is an almost disturbing aftertaste of blood and earth.

'In this wine, we are "drinking Ikaria",' finishes Constantinos, with a melodramatic flourish, signalling the end of the talk.

I get up a bit lightheaded, Ikaria coursing through my veins.

Sharing

I am sitting having breakfast in Thea's Inn with Isa, the ex-wife of my cousin, Dionysios, and her friend, Niki, who grew up in Ikaria and whose mother we will be staying with for a few days.

A few weeks before leaving Australia, I'd Facebook messaged Isa to ask about the island, and she had surprised me by offering to accompany me for part of my trip and bring a friend along. She and Niki tell me they have always wanted to visit the island together, but life had got in the way – children, lack of money, work commitments. This is a sort of pilgrimage for them, a chance to reconnect with the island, and to have a break.

Looking around at the sea across from us, the olive groves below, the whitewashed stones of Thea's Inn, Isa says, 'This is a moment of grace.'

They tell me how when they arrived on the ferry late last night, their hire car had been left waiting for them at the port with their name scribbled on a piece of paper on the dashboard, the keys in the ignition. There was no need for deposits or licences, no suspicion that the car might be stolen. They laugh. It appears nothing much has changed in Ikaria.

'You know we've come to help you discover the island. It was our *obligation*,' says Isa, blue eyes dancing. In a strange twist of fate, it turns out that Isa worked for Urania during the few years she and Dionysios spent on the island. Ikaria is also special to Isa because it was here she was pregnant with their first child.

'I'm not going to check my watch at all while we're here,' declares Niki.

As single mothers, it hasn't been easy for the two friends to leave their children and their jobs to get away for the week. They're determined to make the most of having no responsibilities.

Niki and Isa tell me about meeting in the southern Greek town of Kyparissia several years ago. There they discovered they had both lived on Ikaria at the same time. There is even a photo taken of them together at an Ikarian café, where they'd met by chance, though neither of them remembered the meeting. The photo has since been misplaced. It is clear to me as they tell the almost legendary tale of their friendship that they are very fond of each other.

'We should take another photo at the same café, compare them when we finally find the original,' says Isa.

'Are you joking? There is no way I want to compare myself now to then. Let us remember ourselves as we were,' says Niki.

'I'm happy with myself as I am now,' Isa replies, refusing to let her moment of grace be broken.

Today, the only plan is for us to explore the island. They ask me if there is anything I want to do. I say I am in their hands.

Even after only one day on Ikaria, I realise happily that I'm no longer worried that I might not find what I'm looking for. I feel more relaxed than I have in months, perhaps years. I'm willing to sit back and wait to see what the island offers up.

I ring George after breakfast and he asks about my plans and whether I am closer to discovering the secret to long life. Have I arranged to meet any island elders?

How might I tell him that this morning I was delighted to see a swallow cutting across a clear blue sky? A bee building a tiny hive the size of a coin on the step up to my room? That on my walk yesterday, the heady smell rising from last season's figs underfoot filled me with an inexplicable joy?

I hedge in response to his questions, feeling a twinge of guilt that he is stoking the home fires while I'm spending my days immersing myself in the sensual pleasures of the island. It's hard to explain that I've already started to operate on Ikarian time, letting things unfold as they need to, having faith I will learn what I need to learn.

—

Niki takes the wheel of our hire car, and drives the island's winding roads confidently and fast, cigarette in hand.

We drop in to Urania's office so Isa can say hello to her. Urania is not there, but the woman in the office, Evanggelia, has heard of Isa. She turns to Niki, and after several minutes, they have established a connection. She knows people who know Niki, know who her family is, which town she grew up in.

Back on the road, Niki asks why I have come to Ikaria. I tell her that I read about Stamatis Moraitis a few years ago and have had a fantasy of travelling to the island ever since. I talk about my desire to understand what makes the islanders live so well and so long into their old age, perhaps in a bid to live my own life better, and to reconnect to my own roots in some inexplicable way.

'Did you hear what Evanggelia asked me?' says Niki. 'She said, "*Apo poion eisai?*" – "From *whom* are you?" Everyone belongs to someone, and I think you might find your answer there. Everyone is part of a family, part of a community here. They are part of something bigger than just themselves. No one is ever lost in Ikaria.'

I let that sink in and listen to the happy banter coming from the front as the two friends reminisce. Every twist in the road is a chance for Niki and Isa to reflect: about the house Isa lived in; the strip of beach she walked from to get to the supermarket; the lettuce she craved while she was pregnant with her son in the thick of winter; and the excitement with which the supermarket owner presented her with the first lettuce of the season.

'Everyone looked out for me, slowed their cars on the road to check that I was okay when I was walking, then sped up again,' says Isa. 'The islanders offered me so much food, you wouldn't believe it. And every time I learnt a new word, people rejoiced, particularly if they themselves had taught it to me!' Isa says.

Niki says she has a surprise for us, and drives us to an isolated home with a massive terraced area. She then pulls up to a large taverna, which is closed. Out the back, there are blankets blowing in the wind, a few dogs, and a prolific garden. It looks down on terraces built into the hillside, which tumble almost all the way to the sea.

Niki leaves us for a few moments and we hear laughter. She soon comes back and leads us into the back of the taverna, where the owners live. We walk down a dark, cool corridor into a cha-otic kitchen, where Niki introduces us to her first cousin, Loni, and his wife, Lambrini. We meet their daughter and her fiancé, a handsome couple in paint-splattered clothes, who tell us they are renovating a part of their parents' home to live in after they marry. They currently live in Athens, and have jobs there, but are considering moving back to the island.

Niki and her cousins are ecstatic to see each other, their con-nection evident in their easy banter, even though Niki hasn't visited the island for three years. Lambrini starts placing food on the table: *dolmadakia* (rice wrapped in vine leaves), wild greens, olives, and bread. Every dish is made from ingredients that Loni and Lambrini have grown in their garden. Lambrini serves us a piece of *pasticcio* which she cooked in their wood-fired oven. And tells us we must try the pickled *kritano*, a plant that grows by the sea. After pouring everyone wine, she finally sits down.

Outside, I can see an elderly woman moving around on a walker. Lambrini says this is her 83-year-old mother-in-law, Irini, who lives in another part of the house.

When we compliment the couple on the beauty of their property, Lambrini points to her husband and laughs raucously. 'That's the reason I married him.' It's clear as the discussion unfolds that they've worked the land together, built it up. Now it houses a taverna on the level above, and several rooms for extended family to stay in. Some time ago, they bought the land below from a neighbour and dug it up to create productive fields. Loni owns bulldozers, which he uses to help people around the island dig the hard earth to grow food.

'We can't just live from the taverna,' he says. 'That's forty days of excitement each year, and then there's nothing. We've got to do other things. But the important thing is, we do what we love.'

When Niki tells the family what I am doing on Ikaria, I see Lambrini raise her shoulders as if preparing a speech.

'It's a strange island. I don't know why people might come to Ikaria. If you stopped at the port only, you might turn back again – it's as if there is nothing here. We Ikarians are quite mad. We're always joking. You can't take anything seriously with us.' As if to demonstrate her point, she laughs raucously.

'Ikaria is an emotion, as well as a place. That's why people keep coming back. Ikaria is love,' Lambrini's daughter pipes in. I look at her and her young fiancé, their faces as yet unlined, looking forward to their future together. Their vitality, their energy, is contagious.

'It's a very erotic island. My *yiayia* said that my *pappou*, who was ninety-three at the time, still wanted *it* at least once or twice a week!' says Lambrini, laughing again.

'The women choose the men, not like in other parts of Greece. Traditionally, men had to cut a fig branch with an axe in one swoop to show that they were able to look after a woman. And so, if a woman wanted a particular man, she would present him with a fresh, young branch. If she didn't, she would give him a dry, old branch, which was impossible to cut. And thus, *she* made the choice.'

She talks about the many cultural traditions of the island that helped sustain it in times of poverty; how there was rarely an exchange of money. If you slaughtered your pig, you shared it with your neighbours in a celebration called *heirosfagia*, a communal slaughter. The neighbours would do the same when they slaughtered theirs.

During the winter, villagers would rotate who would host dinner so that householders didn't have to cook each night. You didn't need to call ahead to visit someone. There was a practice of building a communal wall around the villages so that the animals would have a space to graze without getting lost.

'People weren't *atomistes*, individualists. They were socialists without the politics. Poverty makes everyone the same. Money breeds ego. The world would be a better place if more people lived like that. We were hopeful, trusting, looking after each other,' says Lambrini. 'When we needed hope, we went to church, we prayed. Our priests weren't paid, they too worked the fields.' She sounds a bit nostalgic for a time that is fast becoming a thing of the past.

The conversation moves on. They are interested in Australia, have several relatives living there. Lambrini says, 'Now please can you tell me why our Australian relatives who come here, they eat at 6 o'clock and go to sleep so early. Don't they know how to live?'

I laugh, shrug my shoulders. I too have had to change my body clock to 'Greek time' and get used to not eating for long stretches of time. Eating in Greece is so fluid. Meals are guided by what is going on during the day and who you are with. Breakfast often comprises black Greek coffee. Lunch is usually a larger meal in the early afternoon. Dinner, if had, is generally a smaller affair, either at home or out. And it's rarely before 9 pm. Snacking between meals is not common.

I realise that at home I have a low-grade angst about meal times, generally making sure we eat regularly, that we don't eat too late. Now, having meals at regular times now seems so predictable.

'And Australians seem to have so many allergies,' Lambrini complains. 'We could be sitting around the table, and at least a few people have allergies – gluten, fructose, lactose.'

I have often wondered if allergies are our body's natural response to excess – to eating too much processed food made with wheat and sugar, overconsumption of milk and cheese, perhaps too many preservatives and additives in our largely Western diet. I shrug. Who knows?

Lambrini brings an orange and olive oil cake to the table, and *foinikia* biscuits, also made with orange. Setting the *briki* (Greek coffee pot) on the stove to make coffee, she says, 'In the winter when we don't have eggs, we make *foinikia* without them. We listen to the seasons, work with what we have. This one has eggs thanks to our chooks.'

We tell her that we are full, that there is no need to bring more food out.

'Here in Ikaria, we never clear the table when we have guests. And glasses must always be full,' Lambrini says with her trademark laugh.

—

I spot Irini sitting in the afternoon sun on the terrace, and go outside to sit with her. I tell her I am from Australia, am here with her niece Niki.

She tells me that while her husband spent many years in Cleveland in the US, she stayed in a remote nearby village, raising three kids. She says her husband is now ninety-three and is still working the fields.

'It was hard work in those days, my life hasn't been easy. Now I'm old, not so steady on my feet. I fell a few months ago, broke my shoulder.' She points to her shoulder, to the walking frame that she needs to shuffle from her room to the terrace.

She sounds sad, telling me that she hasn't quite been able to recover from losing her eighteen-year-old grandson to a road accident. She looks at me philosophically. 'No matter if you're buried in gold, we all have to pass on sometime.'

Dancing

Over the next few days, I embrace the slower rhythms of the island, waking without an alarm, then indulging in writing in bed each morning. I breakfast on omelettes tossed with home-grown vegetables at Thea's Inn and ring my family. Only then do I meander over to the girls' apartment down the road, where we sit on their balcony, slowly getting ready to go out.

Today, Isa is finishing a watercolour painting of the scene below: a flash of bougainvillea in the foreground and a line of water that winds past a bent tree and into the azure blue sea. We've just made coffee, and are in no rush to go anywhere.

Niki says, 'We need to get there quickly,' putting her runners on and tying her hair back.

We look at her, confused. 'What's the rush today?' Isa asks

'We're going to miss out on the soup,' says Niki, looking at us impatiently, willing us to hurry up.

Isa and I look at each other. It must be *some* soup.

We are heading to one of the many the *panigiria* (village feasts) I've read about – this one is on the site of the church of Saint Isidoros, an isolated little outcrop in the mountains. Niki remembers that the route to the village is a little obscure and worries that our tiny hire car won't make it up the rugged unsealed roads.

'What's so good about the soup?' I ask.

'It's slowly cooked overnight, made from goat meat. And it's delicious. If you go too late, they water it down to accommodate the many people who come. We need to go early.'

Even after a few days, I appreciate how lucky I am to be travelling with a local.

—

When we leave the apartment, the street below is frenetic with activity. It appears that most people in the town are heading up to the feast. Thea has closed the Inn for the day and arranged a bus to take the hospitality students up there. We find Ilias, who tells Niki that the roads to the feast are still unsealed, but assures her that the car should make it.

As our car leaves the bitumen, it bumps wildly on the rocky unpaved roads. Meanwhile, the landscape changes from lush green forest to a barren moonscape peppered with huge Neolithic-style boulders. In the distance the blue sea contrasts with the grey stonescape, stretching out into the horizon. We park behind a long line of cars and start walking down a rocky hill towards the *panigiri*. As I slip and slide down the hill in my open-toed leather thongs, Isa supporting me, I see why Niki wore runners. She walks quickly, her tread as steady as that of a mountain goat. The soup is waiting.

We enter the churchyard through a gate, passing dozens of tables where family groups have already staked a spot. Making our way to the tiny whitewashed church at the end of a path, we light some candles and kiss the icon of Saint Isidoros on his horse.

On the way out of the church, Niki greets the local priest. When he looks at me, as if to question how I'm connected to Niki, I explain that I am a friend, visiting from Australia. I want to ask what the legacy of Saint Isidoros is, what he did, but I'm not sure if it's rude. Instead, I ask if I might take a photo – he cuts a striking figure with his dark, worn robes, standing on top of the stairs smoking a cigarette. He agrees begrudgingly but says that I shouldn't put him on the computer. And though he laughs, I know he means it.

There's already a mass of people, with tables set up in every available space. Niki suggests I find a table while she and Isa get the food. I sit down at a table set out further back in the courtyard, and soon Niki and Isa arrive with a tray laden with forks and knives, plates, a paper tablecloth and a waxed paper package of stewed goat meat, bread, salad and wine. Niki instructs us to put the goat meat on our plates ready for the soup, and soon a smiling man in hi-vis overalls arrives with a metal bucket and a huge ladle. He spoons a fine broth over our meat, all the while chatting and laughing.

I see a few pieces of fat floating around in the soup and the former vegetarian in me cringes. But I needn't worry; the broth is rich and meaty, the flavours deepening with each spoonful. It's comforting, in the same way that the fish soup I ate at the wake after Katerina's funeral was comforting. This is food for the soul. Niki looks at Isa and I expectantly. We nod – it's good. Very good. She looks satisfied. Soon, the man with the ladle comes around again and we fill our bowls for a second time.

I ask Niki if she knows who Saint Isidoros was, what miracles he might have performed. She shrugs. More people arrive, and we move along the benches to accommodate them. I'm squished closer to an elderly gent to my left, and we start talking. His name is Yiorgos, and he asks where I'm from, where my family is from. The man next to him, Antonis, overhears. He's delighted to learn that my father was from a village close to where he was originally from. His whole face lights up, and over the course of the next few hours, he sings out my name periodically, as if I am a long-lost friend. He has married a woman from Ikaria, loves the island dearly, but is clearly proud of his hometown, considers us *patriotes*, compatriots.

I chat with Yiorgos, who tells me how here in Ikaria they travel slowly. And they laugh a lot. 'Why not?' he asks rhetorically. Why not indeed?

The orchestra has started up and I ask Yiorgos if he wants to dance. He says he's probably not up to it; there are too many people on the dancefloor. He tells me about an elderly friend of his who is famous for dancing at the village feasts, putting the young people to shame with his stamina. But this year he was ill. Perhaps if his friend was here, he might be coerced to get up.

'You forget the stress in the dance. But today, I'm happy to sit. But you should dance.'

Squeezing out of my seat, I make my way to the dusty patch of earth that is the dance floor and see that there are a few young women doing the *tsiftedeli*, a belly dance with Balkan and Anatolian influences.

Several of the American students are sitting along a ledge, watching them, wine in hand. It appears they have already had a fair bit to drink, making the most of the more liberal drinking laws in Greece. In the US, many would have to wait until they turn twenty-one. I smile and hold out my hand to them but they shy away, saying they don't know how to do this dance.

'Just feel the music and wiggle your hips,' I say, holding out my hand again.

This time they allow themselves to be drawn down from the ledge. Their eyes shine as they try the moves, swinging their hips to the tribal beats of the music. Two young girls sidle up to us, and I watch them smile encouragingly at the students and show them how it's done.

I've heard so much about the *panigiria* in Ikaria, which now attract tourists from around the world. Urania tells me that traditionally, *panigiria* served to raise money for projects for the town, and everyone came to support them. The rich villagers would generally pay for a simple feast of roast meat, and the poor people would eat. It was a chance for enemies to make peace.

Panigiria occur on the name day of the church to which the village is attached. The villagers give their time voluntarily to support their local *panigiri*. Following the *panigiri,* villagers agree how the proceeds might be best used for a common cause – to help someone who is in hospital or a poor family, to fix part of a road, or to support the school, for example. People from around the island try to come to as many as they can to support each village and town. As well as raising money, they are a chance for villagers to socialise and celebrate. When I spoke to Thea about them, she said that it was remarkable that, what with so many people drinking and dancing all day and night, you rarely saw anyone drunk or fights breaking out. She feels this epitomises what Ikaria is all about.

The number of *panigiria* has grown, with more than two hundred now held on the island. I see myself that there is an atmosphere of joy here – with bands of kids climbing the hill, women chatting as they wait in the queue for the toilet, hundreds of young people talking, laughing and eating. I can't see a single person checking their phones. The only people taking photos are the small number of tourists. The locals are too busy having fun.

Walking up to an area where a band of men – young and old – are cooking, I smile and introduce myself in Greek. 'My name is Spiridoula. I'm from Australia. Do you mind if I have a look?'

Several men hold out their arms in gestures of welcome. They pull me into an enclosed space where a vat that reaches to my shoulders houses the soup we have been eating. They all talk at once about how they have relatives in Australia, mostly in Sydney or Adelaide. It's midday and they explain that they have been at it since the early hours of the morning.

One of the men introduces himself as Yiannis, and I say they are doing great things here.

Yiannis, who has mischievous blue eyes, wipes his brow with a tea towel, looking serious for a moment. 'There's lots of economic problems here in Greece,' he says. 'But we can't put our heads down and get depressed about it. We're fighting it.'

He smiles again, his handsome face crinkling.

I wind my way slowly back to my group, the available space between tables now almost unpassable due to the number of people. Niki is talking to a beautiful young couple, who are here with their two-year-old daughter, Daphne. They tell us they have moved from Athens to Ikaria to give their daughter a simpler life. The young woman has picked up odd jobs, like cutting rags for Ioanna the weaver. She says they are largely vegetarians, but indulge in a little meat on special occasions such as today.

Daphne sits on her mum's lap, picking at the *fava*, a split pea dip they have brought along. She uses her little fingers to pick at the food, like a miniature adult, feeding herself while her parents talk and laugh. I pass her some paper, and Isa gives her some coloured charcoals. Then I draw a picture for her – her own face with huge eyes. She tries to copy it. She shyly makes her way to my side of the table, where I play 'This little piggy' on her fingers. She is delighted.

A tiny friend joins her at the table, and they draw together. Daphne is prolific in her cuddles for her companion, but her little friend pushes her away after one too many. Daphne wanders off to the next table, where more people offer her attention. Her parents are watching out for her, but others are looking out for her too. After more than an hour, Daphne comes back to me and points to her hand. She remembers our game, wants me to play again. As I watch her try and mouth the unfamiliar English words, I marvel at how quickly children learn. Not for the first time, I envy how children grow up here, running and riding their bikes in the countless village squares, organically slotting into the rituals of island life. Daphne's parents echo my thoughts, saying she may choose the excitements of city life later, but they want to offer her a more modest start, so she can learn to appreciate simple things.

It's now late afternoon and I am wedged intimately between Isa and Yiorgos, who insists we must come to his place to eat some fish he's caught himself. Antonis calls out my name – *Spiridoula*, my friend, my compatriot. We all drink more wine, share in the *baklava*, *galaktobouriko* (a custard-filled filo sweet) and *bobota*, a cornmeal and honey sweet I have bought for the table.

As we make to leave, I see that the dance floor is now packed so tightly it's a wonder anyone can move. There are many hundreds of people, with the festivities spilling out of the small church grounds, bodies atop ledges, rocks and every available space. The festivities, we are told, will go on well into the morning.

In the car, Niki tells us she is sated – she got her soup, spoke with some interesting people, saw a few people she hadn't seen for a while. We stop to pick up two older women who are making their way down the mountain, but have somehow missed their lift. Picking up hitchhikers on the island is common practice – we have done it several times already. I listen sleepily as Niki establishes a connection with the women, finds out who they know in common. I'm not surprised. It seems she has some sort of connection with everyone here.

I daydream, thinking about the day's events: the soup, the company, dancing, wine. I've finally experienced an Ikarian *panigiri*, and I too feel sated.

Foraging

A few nights ago, when Thea and I caught up over an impromptu glass of wine and a snatched late-night meal, we found ourselves talking about being daughters. About being the children of first generation migrants. We learnt that we both had strict upbringings in our respective countries of birth, she in the US, I in Australia.

Today, she asks me what my plans are for the day.

'I think I'm going to visit 102-year-old Ioanna – but I can't be sure.' I smile, shrug.

She laughs. 'You can't be sure of anything here.'

It's my turn to laugh. 'I was hoping to meet Ioanna, but the longer I'm here, the more uncomfortable I feel orchestrating such meetings. It seems a bit contrived. Yesterday, when I went to the *panigiri*, I realised it's not just about the old people – it's about everyone, and how they fit in together.'

'That's so true!' says Thea. 'You'll love Ioanna. She's very sharp. She often says to me, "The tourists come, they ask their questions, they take photos, then they leave without buying anything. Is it because I'm too old, or don't they like my work?!"'

'As my daughter would say, "That's just rude." I definitely plan on buying something.'

Everywhere, I am reminded that the islanders need to make a living to supplement the other things they do. The tourist season is all too short.

—

Next I visit Isa and Niki at their studio nearby. Ilias drops by with a little bucket of strawberries from his garden. We eat and talk until midday, then Niki and I decide to head down to the beach. We walk across rough stones, wading through a muddy river and finally making it across the rocks, past a handful of sunbaking tourists, to the sea. Once we skirt the cliffs, Niki gets her knife out to wedge small molluscs from the rocks. She shows me how to pluck edible seaweed from the rock face without damaging the roots. She gently berates me when I don't get it right. We talk about the industry that has arisen of collecting herbs from the mountains. Niki says the elders knew to collect just enough during the season to allow the herbs sufficient time to regenerate. Now, the hillsides are fast becoming stripped of the precious herbs Ikarians have used for centuries to flavour their food and treat their ailments.

By this time, my trousers are soaked, so I take them off and leave them on a rock face. My top becomes wet too, and after a while I discard it and dive into the sea, something I haven't felt like doing for many years. The salty water buoys me, numbs my tongue. Niki says the water is very therapeutic here, and shows me the bucket of sea salt she has collected. 'We won't have to buy any now!' she jokes. I collect seaweed while in the water, the waves drawing me to and from the rocks.

Niki guides me across the river to look for *stamnagathi*, a weed that grows near the sea, and we taste some of the shoots that are hidden in the prickly folds of the plant. It is bitter — we are a few weeks too late. She points out what is edible, and we collect some *kritano* and start heading home. Niki, barefoot, reflects on walking these paths as a child, her step sure on the sharp, slippery rocks. Though she hasn't lived on the island for many years, I get the sense that she is home.

—

It's now mid-afternoon, and we make our way to the village of Christos Raches to visit Ioanna. We find her workshop, which is just out of town, but the doors are closed. I look through the window and see a few large looms and rugs made of tiny colourful rags, just like the ones my grandmother used to make, and vow to come back again.

I pull out a piece of paper with the name 'Nikos' on it, along with his phone number. I had met Nikos's nieces, Dorothy and Lisa, several weeks ago at a café in Melbourne's 'Greek' suburb of Oakleigh. We'd been introduced by a mutual friend, and they'd kindly agreed to tell me about Ikaria. As soon as we met, they toasted the island by having a mid-afternoon glass of wine, 'Just like the Ikarians.'

'The first thing you'll notice when you get to Ikaria is that the whole island is all hills and rock. Nothing is flat except for the airport runway. They had to cut this out of the rock. The flattest part of the island is the soccer pitch. When players kick the ball too hard, it falls into the sea.'

They told me that their elderly father, who also lives in Melbourne, grew up on the island. The sisters visited Ikaria for the first time the previous year and met their father's brother, Nikos, and several cousins. They uncovered a few family secrets too, including that their father's parents had been 'disappeared' for their alleged involvement in the communist movement. Dorothy told me that this had never been spoken about openly in their family.

We ask at a bookshop where we might find Nikos, the priest's son.

'Is he very old?' the bookseller asks. 'The *laographer*?' *Laos* means people, *grapher* is a scribe. A scribe of the people.

Yes, that's the one.

Convoluted instructions follow.

'Do we need to call ahead?' I know the Ikarians are used to having people drop in, but I can't help it. My Aussie manners prevail.

'Are you planning to steal him? I don't think his carer will let you,' the man jokes. 'No, you needn't call ahead,' he adds.

We make our way out of the village along unsealed roads, and are confused when we turn into a dead end.

A van stops beside us, and the driver calls out, 'Where do you want to go?'

'To Nikos, the priest's son.'

'I'll take you there – you'll never find it.'

He takes us up several winding roads a few kilometres outside of the village, then wishes us a good journey.

When we arrive, Nikos's carer comes to the door. She calls Stamatis, Nikos's nephew. He looks confused, but invites us to come in and sit down regardless, asking our business only once we are seated and have been offered refreshments.

Stamatis tells us that 95-year-old Nikos is having an afternoon nap. He informs us that Nikos is still well. He has no blood pressure problems, no cholesterol issues, no heart problems. His appetite is good – he eats everything from lamb to chocolates – and so he should, as he has no health problems to worry about. He's in a wheelchair because he's scared of falling. And yes, it's true that he's a *laographer* – he has published one book and has written another that is soon to be published.

'I'll see if he wants to get up – I think he'll be pleased to see you,' says Stamatis.

Soon after, Nikos comes in. He is wearing a bathrobe and is in a wheelchair, but the word 'cad' instantly springs to mind – perhaps because of the slicked back hair, eyes glinting expectantly, the flirtatious, curious smile.

I let Niki make the introductions. As a native to the island, it's become a running joke between us that everyone she talks to is related by blood or marriage in some way. Once she and Nikos establish several connections, Nikos turns to me and says, 'And who are *you?*'

'I live in Melbourne,' I say. 'And I've come to bring greetings from your nieces, Dorothy and Lisa.'

'You did well, my girl, you did well to come and visit me. Now don't sit so far away. Aren't I lucky to have three lovely young women in my home?' He winks flirtatiously, looks at each of us in turn, clearly enjoying holding the floor. He lights a cigarette and asks if we smoke.

Isa and Niki nod. He looks at me. 'I can tell you don't smoke because your eyes are clear.'

As we spend more time at his table, it becomes apparent that Nikos has honed the art of flirtation. His humour is sardonic, sharp.

As I watch him talk, fascinated, a spaghetti western plays on the television behind him, close-ups of a young Clint Eastwood juxtaposing against Nikos's face. I note that Nikos has fewer wrinkles than both me and Clint, his skin practically unlined.

We ask about his life and he tells us that two of his brothers had to escape their childhood home, alluding to political reasons. No one knows exactly what happened to them, their bodies were never recovered, even after much searching. They left in the middle of the night, and though Nikos had begged to leave with them, they'd said he was too young. He reflects quietly that he was spared, and they weren't. He says his father always wanted to build a chapel on the property to honour their memory. Nikos has now realised his father's dream, with the chapel due to be completed in a few months.

'And I've been to jail you know.' He watches our faces for our reaction.

'Been to jail? What did you do?'

'I burnt a well,' he says, laughing raucously. Then he pauses, a far-off look in his eyes. 'Don't ask. It's best not to reflect on these painful memories.' There is another moment of silence.

As his story unfolds, we piece together that he's been a journalist, working for a notable Athenian paper and living in many countries across Africa and in Beirut. He also studied film and worked as a cinematographer with some notable French directors. He wrote a book about Ikaria, in Ikarian, which drew on many ancient Greek words. He asks Stamatis to bring copies of the book to give to us.

Niki reads out a few passages, remembering words from her childhood. We talk generally about the beauty of the Greek language, and Nikos says that being well versed in language is like 'having a third eye' from which to see the world.

While we're chatting, Nikos turns to his carer, a softly spoken woman originally from Bulgaria.

'Dora, my love, my sweet, please can you get the girls some coffee,' he asks.

'Dora takes care of you,' Isa says.

'And she does a good job of it too. She has seven grandchildren. Two of her sons live in Athens.' He pauses. 'If you had come a few weeks ago, you wouldn't have seen me like this.' He glances at his wheelchair, which he clearly doesn't like being in.

He shrugs philosophically. 'Life is sweet, you still want to live.'

I ask him what his favourite film is.

He pauses, then says: 'The films that move me emotionally. Those about the Depression. Because anyone who has lived through the Depression knows what it means to be starving. To have to get on a boat and leave your country. And to get on that boat not having eaten for days. Would you like to leave your home and get on a boat with nothing except the clothes on your back?'

I confess that I wouldn't.

He lights another cigarette. 'It doesn't matter how *long* life is, but how *entoni*, how intense.'

We worry that we will tire him, but our conversation continues for close to two hours. Finally, we say we should leave to let him rest.

He jokes about what he should write in the books he has given us, then goes around the table, asking each of us what he should inscribe. We make more conversation. I wouldn't put it past him to dawdle so that we might stay longer.

'Is your husband the jealous type?' he asks me.

'Oh yes!' I joke. 'But he doesn't read Greek, so you should write what you want.'

He pauses for several minutes, then asks Stamatis to be the scribe. 'For you, my sweet one, to read in the cold nights of winter, your grandfather, Nikos.'

Stamatis dates it, and passes it to Nikos to sign. Nikos checks the grammar and spelling. While it's not up to his high standards, he lets it go, and signs the book with a flourish. He asks Stamatis to write the same thing for Isa and Niki. To Niki's, he adds, 'and to connect with your culture.'

'Now, I have keys to the house next door,' he says, picking them up from an ashtray and holding them up, his eyes teasing flirtatiously. 'Why don't you stay there?'

'We can't. Perhaps next time.'

He looks sad for a moment. 'Don't leave it too long.'

As we make our way from the property, we pass a stately war memorial with many Ikarian names on it. Meanwhile, Nikos and Dora are at the window, waving us off all the way to the car.

—

We make our way down to Christos Raches again and decide to get a bite to eat. We go into a shop that makes pizzas and snacks. It quickly becomes clear that Niki knows the owner; she once dated her brother when she was in high school. Isa and I exchange glances. Is there anyone she isn't connected to here?

Niki's friend heats up food, offers us syrupy deserts she has prepared from local fruit, and sits down with us as we eat our pizza and rolls.

Niki quickly catches up on who is doing what, who has had kids, who is still unmarried.

Her friend is impressed that we are three mothers taking a trip alone. 'Escaped from Alcatraz. Lucky you!' she exclaims. 'As a working mother, you never get a moment of peace. In the summer, we keep this place open 24/7. It's hard. Who has time to go to the beach?'

We talk about several young people who've moved to Christos Raches from Athens. She says some of them don't last.

'They think it's easy living off the land, making a go of it. But it's not. To keep your house warm in the winter, you need to cut firewood two times a week, if you can find it. The garden doesn't produce much in the cold months. You need to work at it. But of course, there are the benefits – clean air, a safe place for your kids to grow up, real food.

'I had it hard as a kid. I was orphaned early, had to work, practically brought me and my brother up by myself. I remember I wanted a pair of runners, Nikes. They cost more then than they do now. I saved up for those runners for months, and when I wore them, I was so proud. I had very little, but I appreciated what I had.'

When the conversation moves on to our children, she says she doesn't want her adult children to work until they've finished university. It's seen as slightly shameful when a parent sends their child out to work. What will people say, that their parents can't support them?

I say that in Australia, kids are encouraged to have a job from an early age, so they can have a bit of independence, and some pocket money.

'Is it true that Australian parents tell their kids they must leave home once they turn eighteen?' she asks, looking mortified.

'It used to be more prevalent,' I say, 'but now kids can't afford to leave home so early because house prices in cities are so high. At any rate, my parents didn't want me to leave home until I got married!'

'It's natural for kids to get independence, for couples to move in together, but there has to be a balance,' she replies.

We spend a good hour with Niki's friend and buy several jars of her sweets. We then go to another café, order a beer, and watch parents and young children move around the square. A tiny basketball ring has been set up, kids ride their bikes up and down the square and someone calls out to a neighbour as the sun sets on the village. It feels like a scene in a movie, and I sit back, watching contentedly.

Accepting

The days bleed one into another, time seeming to stretch and contract languidly. Isa and Niki find out that the ferry back to Athens is on strike on the day that they planned to leave – they are obliged to extend their trip. It's as if the island is conspiring to keep them here, just like the Sirens entrapped Odysseus and his men. Happily, they allow themselves to be seduced for a few more days by the island's charms.

After another slow start to the day, we set off to drink from the 'immortal waters' gushing out of a wind-beaten rock on one side of the island, our hair whipping wildly about us. Then we have coffee in a little taverna overlooking the sea, and visit an isolated monastery that is a few hundred years old. The young monk there looks a little bewildered when I buy some incense and a vigil lamp as a gift for Mum, handing me a note in change that looks as if it's been sitting under a rock for the last decade. Winding our way through the mountains, we go in search of Pigi village to sample the famous honeyed donuts, *loukoumathes* and to see the Chapel of Theoskepasti, which has been carved inside a cave, covered with a giant rock. Isa is keen to see if the donuts are still as good as she remembers them.

After visiting the low-roofed chapel with its dark and delicate old icons, we head down to wait outside a tiny room. A woman is heating a large vat of oil. We chat with her while she pulls back the towel on a tub of loose dough and drops a few spoonfuls of it into the hot oil. The donuts sizzle up seductively. When they are cooked, the woman removes them from the oil, drains them on some paper, and drizzles them with dark honey. We make our way to long wooden tables that overlook the fields below, and feast on our sweet bounty.

'They're amazing,' I say. 'But are they as good as you remember them?'

'They're just as good,' Isa says as she wipes away the last of the viscous honey from her plate.

—

It's after 10 pm by the time we return from our day's outings and I'm looking forward to going to bed with a book I've borrowed from a rickety bookshelf in Urania's office.

'What about a drink at Thea's?' says Isa, who still has a bit of energy left.

Given the tavern is just downstairs from my room, I think that one drink can't hurt. I'm conscious of making the most of every opportunity while I'm away from home. Going out for a spontaneous drink late at night doesn't feel possible back in Melbourne. Waking, eating and going out whenever I want has been liberating. Niki and Isa are also rejoicing in being child-free. We all have teenage children, and they appear to be coping in our absence.

Earlier this morning George and I had our daily Skype chat, in between sending each other several text messages throughout the day.

'I'm really glad you've made this trip, and I want you to keep having a good time. But we miss you a lot,' he said.

'I miss you too, darling. I'm having a great time, but it's because I know I'm coming home in ten days.' I feel as if I have been in Greece for months, yet the past few weeks have passed so quickly.

'We need to travel more, even if it's just locally,' George mused. 'We get too caught up here. I can't believe how much it takes to run the house. It's never-ending. You finish with something, and there's always something else.'

I spoke to Dolores too and she told me how her team lost in basketball, that she'd enjoyed watching the school production a few nights back, and that she is doing her homework. She told me she misses me.

'I miss you too, darling,' I'd replied. 'I keep seeing things that I think you would love, that I want to share with you. I don't think I want to go away without the family for this long again.'

'You've done it now, Mum – and you can do it again if you need to. But that doesn't mean we don't miss you.'

'You're a wise young woman, Dolores.'

'Yes, that very true!' she'd said, laughing.

Emmanuel had then got on the phone and said he missed me too, and I should just come home 'right now!'

'I'm going to give you a hug!' he'd added, squishing the phone to his chest.

Isa's children have also been providing her with regular updates, including a tale about chasing a mouse around the house, and having to set up ever-more complicated traps for it. Niki's daughter has spent time at her father's house, has eaten too much souvlaki, and is now back home, safe and sound, with a neighbour looking in on her. All is well. Everyone is surviving without us.

We make our way inside the Inn, and Thea brings us some of her husband's homemade wine. It's strong, tasting of berries and earth. We ask Thea to join us and she orders *tsipouro,* a strong spirit made from the residue of the grape press. When the waitress brings her a generously filled glass, Thea balks at the size. The waitress laughs and says that it's mostly ice.

Thea tells us that she came to Ikaria several times as a child and teenager to visit family. When she met Ilias, now her husband, on the island, her mother refused to let her return to Ikaria – she'd wanted Thea to marry and live in the US. Watching Ilias move around the place – assured, relaxed – I can't imagine him living anywhere else. These days, Thea travels regularly to the US to visit her ageing mother.

Her children, who are in their twenties, help in the family business, work their father's farm, and hang around the island with their friends. Thea says her oldest son – whose *tsipouro* she is drinking – is an Ikarian 'body and soul', and doesn't ever want to leave the island. I've seen Thea's eldest around the place, a tall bearded young man who caught the attention of the young hospitality students. I could hear them giggling under my window each night as they flirted with him and several of the other local boys. The morning the students were leaving, I heard them ask him to stay in touch through Facebook. He politely declined, telling them he didn't much *do* Facebook.

Thea says that her youngest son recently visited the US, stayed with family, and worked for a stint. After initial resistance, he came to like it there. She would like him to go back to expand his horizons.

'The young people here are too relaxed. It's like "What will be, will be",' says Thea. 'But I want my sons to travel, keep their options open, open their eyes a bit.'

'To be so sure of what you want at his age, to know that you are part of a place, isn't that a good thing?' I ask Thea. It feels rare to meet young people who know exactly what they want, who aren't dissatisfied with what they have.

'It's good on one hand,' she replies, 'but on the other I want my sons to have some sort of focus, maybe study abroad and think about their future.' She talks about how the options for work are limited on the island: mostly some tourism in the summer months, and working the land. Though Thea has a strong American accent, I sense she's become very much Ikarian in her years here. She has a fierce mother spirit, a need to do the best for her offspring.

The conversation prompts Niki to talk about her dilemma – should she come back to the island and try to make a go of a life here, or set up a new life in Australia, where her parents had once migrated?

'I know what I would do. Go to Australia,' says Thea.

Niki looks doubtful. Returning to the island after a three-year absence has reminded her how much she loves it. In the last few days, I've watched her pick flowers by the side of the road, cherries from a mountain top, herbs by cliff faces. She's reconnected with her mother, with neighbours and with family friends. She's driven the winding roads confidently, told an errant driver off passionately and quickly established connections with everyone she's met. If there is something distinct about being Ikarian, Niki personifies it: fierce, generous, passionate and proud.

While her mother lives on the mainland most of the year, her family still owns some land here. Over coffee, Thodoris planted the seed of an idea in her mind to set up a small canteen overlooking a spectacular cliff that plunges into the sea. But it's risky. She is a single mother with no capital. What would she do during the winter months when half the island moves back to Athens and there are hardly any tourists?

And then there's her fourteen-year-old daughter to consider.

'I would love to live on the island, but what would my daughter do?' says Niki. 'There are a few schools here, but I couldn't offer her the drumming lessons she loves, nor tutoring. I wouldn't be able to give her the type of thing I offered my son.' Niki's son is now studying robotics and Japanese in Crete. The opportunities in his line of work internationally are good, whereas in

Greece they are limited. Like many thousands of the country's young people, he will be compelled to look for work elsewhere.

In talking it through with us, and after days of indecision, I think Niki has finally found the bottom line – she is a mother, and she will sacrifice what she wants to give her daughter a better future, just as her parents did before her.

Thea brings another carafe of wine – on the house – and we drink and talk into the small hours of the night. My book will have to wait.

—

The next day we head off to stay with Niki's mother, Stella. She has just arrived from Athens to spend the summer months in her native village of Ploumari. Without yet having met me, she lets me stay in her home, along with Niki and Isa. I come to call her Kyria Stella – Mrs Stella. She is stout, practical, warm.

On our first day in the village, we walk down to the local cemetery to light a candle for Niki's dead father. We see a middle-aged family friend of Niki's drinking *tsipouro* at his son's grave; his young son died in a car accident on the island. There is another man there building a fiddly monument to his mother. Later that night, when a black inkiness has settled around the village, we hear voices coming from the cemetery as more people join the mourners to chat and drink.

I can't help but think about how sudden, random acts can take life from us. Everyone I have met on the island seems to know someone who has drowned, had a car accident on the roads, or come to a tragic end through a freak mishap. Death seems closer here. It's more personal. There's an almost daily reminder that we might be robbed of life suddenly. Perhaps this knowledge helps the locals enjoy each moment, each day.

—

Over the next few days, Stella cooks meals for us while we tour the island like irresponsible teenagers. When we get home, she presents us with steaming plates of *dolmathakia* made from the vine leaves we picked from nearby fields; string bean and goat stew; *pasticcio*.

At the dinner table, I listen as Niki exchanges gossip and news with her mother – which uncle has passed on, which woman has gone a little mad, which child is running wild. The names and descriptions wash over me, making me think of the smallness of the village – everyone knows everyone. Niki points out once again that no one is ever *lost* in Ikaria. While this means that the islanders look after each other, it also means that it's hard to keep a secret.

During the day, neighbours and relatives drop in sporadically, bringing something from their gardens – eggs, lettuce, vine leaves. An elderly neighbour – wild hair akimbo and voice booming – reads our coffee cups for us. After she leaves, we hear her screaming to her grandson down the street to come in and *eat something*. In the evenings, we watch the Greeks compete against the Turks in a friendship round of *Survivor* on television, a show that Kiria Stella confesses she is addicted to.

We watch the news, hear about new taxes being introduced, Syrian refugees still streaming in from the Turkish coast onto islands near Ikaria: Kos, Chios, Lesbos and Samos; most moving through, others choosing to try their luck in Greece.

I think about the conversations I've had with young Greeks, about how hard it is to leave your home unless you have few other choices. I imagine how difficult it must have been for my parents to leave their scenic villages, their passports stamped 'labourer', then try to make a living from working in factories in a new country, all so that their children might have a better future. And I think about how lucky I am to have a place I can call home.

Thanking

Today, Isa, Niki and I set off for the main port town of Agios Kirikos, where we go into the tourist office and ask for Urania's father, Nikos. While Urania runs the branch of the family tourist business in Armenistis, Nikos still helps run the Agios Kirikos branch.

It's been eighteen years since Isa last saw Captain Nikos – her former boss – and I watch as he hugs her warmly, clearly very fond of her, and exclaims that it's been too long. 'Isa *mou*, my Isa, you haven't changed a bit,' he says, pulling up a few seats for us, and sitting down at his desk, facing Isa.

'I never did thank you properly, Isa *mou*. Your "Wild West" program went so well. Remember how we never thought it would take off? Well, it made us a lot of money and that's all due to you.'

Isa looks pleased at the compliment; she had not realised she'd left a legacy on the island. She had doubted that Urania or her father would even remember her.

Meanwhile, Niki and I are confused about what on earth the Wild West program was. Nikos explains that it was a tour that involved a convoy of jeeps careening down the rough western side of the island. At the time, the roads were unsealed. We drove the very same route yesterday, and the spectacular plunging cliffs, isolated stone houses barely clinging to barren rock faces, and dogs tied to the side of the road to keep the goats under control had scared me. The small whitewashed church-shaped tributes at the side the of road attested to the many road accidents that had happened. And despite the mild weather, the wind battered the waves wildly against the cliffs. In the winter, it would have been bitterly cold here. Niki told me that electricity only came to the area a few decades ago. The children travelled to school by boat. And yet the villagers who lived here survived and even prospered.

'Allow me the honour of taking you out for a coffee,' says Nikos.

We make our way a few doors down to a café overlooking the harbour. Isa and Nikos talk about the changes to the town, the new eateries and houses that have been built higher up the hill, the appearance of a graded path along the harbour.

Like many Greeks I have met, Nikos is something of an orator. He speaks passionately of the long history of the island, the Ionian roots of its residents, of a proud history of education and philosophy. Standing up, he recites the national anthem for us, and a few excerpts from Sophocles' *Antigone* for good measure, "Tomorrow is tomorrow/Future cares have future cures/And we must mind today." This is one of the key principles that guides his life.

As he moves on to other subjects, Nikos says, 'On several occasions, while I was commandeering a ship, I would hear my father's voice warning me. I can't explain it, but he saved me on several occasions from crashing into cliffs, woke me when we were at risk of colliding into another boat. Saint Nicholas was the patron saint of sailors. That's why so many of us are called Nicholas on the island. We knew that the sea posed a danger to our lives, and so we didn't idolise wealth and material things. Instead, we valued life, lived for the moment.

'But really our wives were the heroes, the ones who were both mothers and fathers back at home. They knew the dangers of the sea, and most loved and adored their husbands. They looked us in the eyes when we came home.'

As if on cue, he is interrupted by a phone call from his wife, who he talks with warmly. When he hangs up, he says that marriage is about connection, not about a piece of paper.

He tells me proudly that as a captain of a ship, he has travelled the world and been to Australia twenty-eight times. 'But my favourite place was New Zealand,' he adds. 'What impressed me is that they support their farmers, give them tax breaks. That's a sign of a healthy society, a country that rewards the people who grow the food. And it's so beautiful – whoever wrote about paradise, they were definitely thinking about New Zealand.'

At eighty-one, Nikos still has his own desk at the tourist office, keeps his own hours and loves what he does.

'What would I do at home? To give something to your work, you need to love it. I didn't call myself a captain, I called myself a traveller. Even now I still travel.

'When I came back to the island after I finished with the ships, I was very stressed because I had become used to the rigorous systems of ship life. In the tourist office, I would organise transfers, but my drivers simply wouldn't rock up. Most of the time, they would have gone for a swim, or drunk themselves into oblivion, or they had simply forgotten. Once, one of my drivers left a group of tourists sweltering in the August sun while he was eating *baklava* at a local café around the corner. The laidback attitude of the islanders drove me crazy. I was so stressed I had a heart attack.' He laughs, hits his chest. 'Now I'm used to it.'

He admits he made some mistakes and expresses regret that his children grew up largely without him. He first met his son when he was eighteen months old. When Urania was born, he received a telegram at some isolated overseas port where he was stationed, saying that he was the father of a girl. He thought it was a joke and ignored it because he had wanted a son. He tells us he met Urania when she was three months old, and didn't want much to do with her. Then, one day, his mother brought her into the room and put her on his belly, and Urania started laughing. Nikos says that was the day the ice thawed, the day he fell in love with his daughter.

While Nikos admits pushing Urania into studying economics, he says proudly that she also completed a degree in fine arts – and that her painting of Icarus hangs at the University of Minnesota.

We talk about the Ikarian phenomenon of longevity, and how inexplicable it is. He tells us about a 106-year-old man who died only last year. Nikos says the man's mind was so much sharper than his own, even if his body was starting to fail him.

'I'm a realist. I know the cycle of life, even if I have a small angst about dying. The secret to living a full life is to have a good time, and to see your children do well in their lives. If we feel love inside us, we can send it out and get it back. And we are obliged to offer something to ourselves, to look after ourselves.'

We embrace Captain Nikos, thank him for the coffee and step out into the spring sunshine.

—

'I have a strange question,' I tell Thea the next morning.

She braces herself a little. I don't think she knows what to make of me.

'You know of Stamatis Moraitis, from the *New York Times* article?'

She nods.

'Do you know where he is buried?' I ask.

She looks at me quizzically and says that she doesn't. I explain that I want to find his grave before I leave Ikaria, light a candle to keep his memory alive, and say thanks for inspiring this journey.

'No one has ever done that before, Spiri. It's a nice gesture. I don't doubt you will find it.'

I am not so sure. I've seen many gravesides dotted on isolated hills and rocky outcrops along the island. Many hold not more than a few dozen graves, and are off tracks that aren't easily accessed. Stamatis's grave could be anywhere.

Captain Nikos had not been sure where Stamatis's resting place was either – he'd waved somewhere in the distance, thought it might be in the hills out of town.

I've had a wonderful time with Niki and Isa, so I'm sad they are leaving this afternoon. Going back to Kiria Stella's to say goodbye, I discover she has been quietly working on my problem. She has made several phone calls and has found out that Stamatis is buried not more than a kilometre away from where she lives. Niki knows the cemetery, and says that we have time to go there before she and Isa must leave for their flight.

Before she farewells us, Kiria Stella packs me a bottle of oil, some wicks to light the vigil lamp, some jars of honey and a tub of *pasticcio*. She refuses to accept my gifts for her hospitality, and makes me promise to drop by before I leave Ikaria.

I am touched once again by how willing everyone is to help me out.

We turn off the main road, and head down an unsealed road that winds down to the sea. We nearly miss the turn-off to the cemetery, but a small sign alerts us that we are at the right place: 'Do not litter, this is a sacred site,' says a sign leaning against a rusted car that has been dumped along the road.

A plateau has been dug into the mountain, and it holds a burial site with several rows of graves. The blue-hued mountain looms over the tiny cemetery, an old gate with a cross on it barely able to hold back the forest from taking it over again.

Niki and Isa go on ahead, searching for Stamatis's grave. I lag behind, looking at the fading photos, noting names and dates. For such a small graveyard, there are a disproportionate number of people born last century who died only recently.

The girls have found the grave, and I join them. It's a simple white marble tomb, covered in dried branches and seeds. I brush away the foliage and see that Stamatis died at ninety-eight. The headstone cavity holds a glass with a candle in it, and a small, fading photo of Stamatis from the *New York Times*. I can't help but smile at his open, willing expression as he squints into the sun, leaning on his shovel. While his story helped make the island famous for the longevity of its residents, he is buried simply, like everyone else here.

Unable to find a holder for the wick, I must be content with simply lighting the candle. We leave the oil and wicks behind. Perhaps the next person who comes here will find something to light the vigil lamp.

As we make our way out of the cemetery, Niki points out the graves of some people she knew. 'This was my father's godfather. And this was an uncle. I remember this person, they were this high ...' She puts her hand to her chest, remembers the amusing nickname that captured how short he was.

As she narrates her anecdotes, the names on the graves begin to mean something more than just impressive ages engraved on marble and stone. The people buried here had personalities; they were part of families; they worked their land. Many saw their children leave for distant shores. They experienced several wars, would have faced hunger and political unrest. They cried and laughed, gossiped and feasted. Some lived longer, some less. But they all eventually died, just as we all will. I realise that the thought doesn't depress me anymore, as it did when my friend Katerina died. This is simply how it is. This is life.

As Niki and Isa make their way back to the car, I return to check Stamatis's grave one more time, place a hand on the cool marble and say goodbye.

Isa and Niki stop outside the new apartment where I'll be staying for a couple of days in the village of Armenistis. After helping me hitch my luggage up several flights of stairs, they admire the view and the ample kitchen, and smoke a cigarette. Back down at the car, we hug tightly. It feels as if we've been travelling together for months, not a little over a week. We have all got something out of this trip, and Niki and Isa didn't want it to end – but they are now ready to go home to their children – as am I.

As soon as Niki and Isa drive off, I wonder if I will be lonely here by myself. Perhaps I should try and make my way to the festival that's on a few villages along, surround myself with people, keep doing things to make the most of my time here. But I catch myself and my need to keep 'doing' all the time. I realise that despite how much I've enjoyed the company of Isa and Niki, I'm looking forward to having some time to myself, a chance to reflect on all that has happened in the past few weeks.

It feels comforting to unpack and hang my clothes, do my washing, and gather together the marmalades, honey and ouzo I have bought as gifts. I'm tempted to make a list of who I still need to buy for, but resist – I haven't made a list in three weeks, and I'm holding off doing so for as long as possible.

It's my birthday tomorrow and I imagine eating alone *will* feel a little lonely. I respond to an email from Urania, invite her and her husband out for a meal tomorrow to celebrate with me.

I video call my family, keen to connect with them after a few days of hurried phone calls and no wifi. I show them my sea view and around the apartment. George quips that he paid twice as much to stay in a highway hotel in regional Victoria for work recently. It had a very fine view of the carpark.

George also fills me in on the latest, including a few appointments we need to attend on my return. I get out my diary for the first time in three weeks, scribble the commitments in. Organising my life in this way feels familiar, even strangely comforting. George sounds a little tentative, as if he is worried about interrupting me with the minutiae of our life. Perhaps he thinks now that I've had a heady taste of freedom, I might find family life in Melbourne boring.

'Don't worry, I won't get all depressed on you when I come back,' I say. 'Unless of course the weather is horrid.'

He laughs, sounding relieved. 'So, what can we expect will be different about you?'

'Well, I'm drinking Greek coffee in the morning. Not snacking as much. Eating lots of greens every day. Tell the kids to watch out – there will be wild greens with every meal.

'People mostly move to work their fields or do their housework. As I've had no housework, I've done a lot of sitting, eating and socialising. With the odd bit of berry picking in between. I'll be doing a lot more walking when I get home …

'And I might put it to the neighbours that we should set up a park bench in our street, like in *Theio* Spiro's street! Imagine if every street had a park bench where people could talk to each other?' I laugh, wondering what the local council would make of that idea.

We speak for a good length of time and then I hang out some clothes before heading off for a coffee and a spinach pie downstairs. I chat to the owner, whose daughter and friends have just come by the café. She rolls her eyes when they leave, says they're keen to swim – don't they know that the water is freezing? *Children simply never listen.*

Next, I walk down to the supermarket to buy things I can't easily find in Melbourne, such as goat's milk yoghurt; *Kathoura*, a traditional Ikarian cheese; and a spiced honey sesame cake. I also buy more Ikarian honey, this time with walnuts floating in it, to give as gifts back home. I force myself to put down a bottle of wine with an image of Icarus on it – I must be close to reaching my luggage limit.

Back at the apartment, I sit on my balcony and watch the streetscape below. The shopkeeper's children are swimming in the sea, people are calling out to each other from across the street, and bulldozers are trying to fix roads that seem to be forever in a state of disrepair. A rickety truck on three wheels goes by, several mopeds, women with shopping bags. I watch as a man escorts an elderly couple to a car. It's difficult to feel lonely in a place like this.

Niki's words echo in my mind – *no one is ever lost in Ikaria.*

Celebrating

I wake up on my forty-seventh birthday and put some coffee on, then go outside to check on my clothes. It rained last night, and the famed *Meltemi*, the northerly wind I've read about, is blowing wildly. There weren't enough pegs, and most of my clothes are strewn in a puddle on the ground. I can see a few of my under-clothes on the balcony below. A pang of loneliness hits me. At home, my family would be greeting me with cake and coffee in bed, singing me happy birthday. Here I start my birthday by try-ing to get my soggy clothes dry.

I go back inside, and feel better after my first sip of coffee. I eat half a tub of goat's milk yoghurt. A piece of Kiria Stella's *pas-ticcio* is left in the fridge. I sing silently to myself, 'It's my birthday and I'll eat *pasticcio* if I want toooo … for breakfast if I want toooo …' I know I'm not hungry, that the *pasticcio* is comfort eat-ing. I feel a little sick afterwards.

I turn on my laptop and already there are several messages from family, and a few dozen birthday messages on Facebook. As I start responding, a video call comes in from George. There's a bit of fiddling around, and then he and the kids sing happy birthday to me, cut me a green tea cake with candles, don home-made birthday hats. I make a show of blowing out my candles through the computer. They tell me I must make a wish. *I wish to return safely*.

After we finish the call, I spend more time on Facebook.

A few hours later, I realise the weather has cleared and berate myself. I am on a lovely island and I've spent the morning on my laptop.

I decide to walk to Thea's and perhaps finally talk with her about the Blue Zones phenomenon. But first, I will drop in to Urania's office, just down the road.

Urania is in, and with her is Ines, a German woman who has big blue eyes and a mop of curly grey hair. Ines is forthright and friendly, and I like her immediately. She tells me she worked with Urania and Isa eighteen years ago and met her Belgian partner while on the island during that time. They are now here on holidays, coincidentally staying a few doors down from where we were staying in Nas.

Ines and I listen as Urania talks about the island, the projects that should be carried out to make the beaches safer, how signs need to be put up at the thermal springs for those with health problems, how a park should be made for the children. She has come to loggerheads with legal bodies when she's taken action herself and has retaliated, giving them a piece of her mind. It's clear her need to make the island a better place is causing her stress. I tell her that it sounds as if she is carrying the island on her shoulders, like the Titan god Atlas.

'Things have got to be done, Spiri. And I don't have children, so I put my energy into the island.'

I recognise her stress, which resembles my own during busy work periods. Both Ines and I implore her to look after herself, telling her she will be more effective if she herself is well.

When Ines says she is heading to the women's cooperative in Christos Raches, I leap at the opportunity to go with her and see if Ioanna's workshop is open, perhaps visit Nikos one more time. Now that I am without a car, I am much less mobile. Once I'm in Christo, it's only a short taxi ride from there.

Ines is happy give me a lift up the mountain. Saying goodbye to Thea will have to wait.

We walk past Ioanna's workshop. It is closed again. Perhaps my fantasy of chatting to her and learning to weave with her may not come to pass – but I have had so many experiences here already, I am not disappointed.

We make our way to a spring, where Ines fills her bottle with water. Then we sit for coffee at the women's cooperative. Ines tells me she is very interested in brain training as a way of preventing dementia – coincidently, the things she advocates are similar to the things the Ikarians already do – managing their blood pressure and sugar levels through activity and diet, and keeping their brains and bodies active by doing the things they enjoy as part of their everyday routines. She is considering setting up a business running programs to this effect. She says the problem is that most people don't want to think about dementia until they have it. But by then, it's too late for prevention.

I tell Ines about my interest in longevity, about my observation that the elders on the island have been through many difficulties – hunger, war, deprivation. Ines notes that research shows that overall calorie reduction is a proven longevity factor. I share with her that I had *pasticcio* for breakfast. She laughs. We agree that the important thing is to live as well as we can for as long as we can.

I tell Ines about Nikos, and how I'd like to see him again. She waits while I call him, ready to give me a lift back to my apartment if I need it.

'*Kirie* Nikos, it's Spiridoula here. How are you?'

'I'm well,' he replies cheerfully. 'And much better now that you called. I said to Stamatis not more than a ten minutes ago, "Those nice girls that visited last week, they haven't even rung me. They've forgotten me already …" And here you are.'

'Don't worry, we haven't forgotten you. You made a great impression on us. In fact, I'm in Christos Raches and was hoping to visit you. Is that okay?'

'Of course, of course. I'll send Stamatis to get you.'

'Don't worry, I'll take a taxi.'

We pay for our coffee and the shop attendant rings me a taxi. I chat to the taxi driver, who tells me Kirios Nikos is an old friend of his. When we arrive at Nikos's house, the taxi driver comes in for a coffee.

Nikos is waiting at the table – dressed, hair combed, looking expectant. Stamatis wanders in from the garden.

'Dora, Dora *mou*, where are you?' calls Nikos.

Dora duly comes from the kitchen, and Nikos asks her to make coffee.

'How are you, Nikos?' the taxi driver asks.

'Well, as you can see, not as good as I was,' he says wryly, casting his eyes to the wheelchair. 'But let's not talk about me. How are you?'

The taxi driver talks about his wife, his children. Not long after, he gets up to go, his coffee unfinished. He looks a little uncomfortable. I get the impression he hasn't seen Nikos for a while; perhaps he is disconcerted by the wheelchair.

Once the taxi driver is gone, Nikos turns to me. 'I'm happy you're here. I really thought you girls had forgotten me.'

I tell him Isa and Niki have gone home to their children. I say that Niki intends to call him.

'And you, you're not leaving again, you will stay here, right!' He looks to the keys sitting in a bowl. 'Take your pick – do you want to stay at the apartment next to the house, or the one at the beach?'

'That's very kind,' I reply with a laugh. 'But I too will soon have to go home to my children, my husband ...'

'You didn't tell me you had a husband ...'

'Oh, I believe I did ...'

'If things were different, I would be making you another offer ...' He looks at me evenly with a whisper of a smile, as if propositioning a woman half his age is the most natural thing in the world.

'My husband is waiting for me at home.' I too smile, am the first to look away.

Stamatis and Dora fumble around the kitchen, preparing lunch. There is no question of my not staying.

I navigate the conversation around to Nikos's health. He tells me dismissively that he has a brain aneurism, which impacts his balance. It's not worth removing; the operation is too dangerous for a man his age.

He adds, philosophically, '*Kai ta kala kathoumena, kai ta kaka.*' (We must expect the good with the bad.)

Stamatis brings in four bowls of *fava* – a thick yellow split pea soup drizzled with olive oil – and some homemade bread and olives.

'We used to eat this when I was a child. It lined our empty stomachs ...' Nikos says.

Indeed, the soup is very thick and filling.

We talk about the chapel that is nearly finished and I tell Nikos I would like to see it before I leave.

'Stamatis will show you,' says Nikos. 'He's been doing good work out there – reviving the old chicken coop, making a vegetable garden, bringing life back to the property ...'

Stamatis talks about his fond memories of visiting Uncle Nikos as a child; how much he still enjoys being here. During lunch, his wife calls; the line drops out and he shrugs. His wife and daughter live in Crete. I can't help but wonder why he is here. He tells me that working the land makes him feel peaceful and is good for his health. I don't ask any more questions.

Finally, by mid-afternoon, I tell Nikos that I should go and let him get some rest. He tells me Stamatis will show me around outside, and then take me back to my apartment.

'Are you sure you don't want to stay?' he asks again, dangling the keys. 'The house is just sitting there, waiting for you …'

'Perhaps next time I come. Thank you for your generosity. When I get back to Melbourne, Dorothy, Lisa and I will give you a call.'

Stamatis takes me outside, and we walk along the uneven ground, across to an old outhouse that was once the main home. At the entrance, an antique stove sits in the sun. Inside, a cooler box like one my grandmother had sits on an old table set on the dirt floor. Simple cast-iron kitchen implements are stacked neatly in corners. This two-room home is much simpler than the one next door, but at more than a hundred years old, it's still standing. Stamatis winds me around the garden, shows me neat rows of vegetables. He takes me to the original chicken coop, with he says is palatial compared to most he has seen. He has revived the roosting section, and cleared the three-metre run connecting the chook's sleeping area.

He opens the door to the laying section, where a small egg sits, saying, 'I bought the new chicks, and within a day they had found the run, knew where to lay. Instinct is a wonderful thing …'

Finally, he takes me down to the chapel, a pristine white building that gleams in the afternoon light.

'It's huge,' I say 'I hadn't expected it to be so big. Nikos must be very proud that it's nearly finished. What a great legacy to leave …'

'Yes, I think he's proud. And sad. Proud that he did it, but sad that he is getting too old to enjoy it, that it took so long. He doesn't like not being able to walk as much as he did, doesn't like that his body is failing him. In his heyday, he and his brothers used to be such flirts …

I can only imagine what a flirt Nikos was in his youth. I see that he is still hopeful that he will have more years of life, but sad too that he no longer feels like his former self.

We make our way to the car, where Dora joins us so that she can come down and buy some sweets from the shop below my apartment. We make our way silently down the mountain, each of us in our own thoughts.

—

Later that evening, I look at myself in the mirror – familiar hazel eyes stare back at me, a mess of wavy brown hair, scarlet painted lips. It's not often that I stop at my reflection in the mirror, except to hone in on the little lines settling around my eyes and lips. But today, I tell myself that I look okay for my forty-seven years. I think back to the three-word purpose list I made a few years ago. *Family. Health. Creativity.* My family is well looked after. Soon I will be back with them, where I belong, where I am needed. We are all healthy. And I am lucky enough to be on an exquisite island with the freedom to explore and question and write. I feel vital, content. I slip on a jacket, grab my bag and head out of the apartment to meet Urania and Thodoris for dinner.

Urania is waiting downstairs, laden with packages. She compliments me on my dress, kisses my cheek and hands me a bowl of *koukia* (broad beans), she has cooked with wild white fennel and tomato sauce. I'm confused – aren't we going out to eat? Yes, her friend Marianthi, who runs a restaurant, has some options for us to choose from, but it's still early in the season, the restaurant is not yet *properly* open … She lets the sentence hang, leaving me wondering if the only thing we will be eating tonight is *koukia.*

As we walk up the stairs to the restaurant, Urania points to the whitewashed floor underfoot that's designed to make the terrace look like cobblestones. She tells me this is her work, done when Marianthi first opened the restaurant and couldn't afford to decorate. She points to the sign with the restaurant's name, 'Baido', and tells me the artwork is hers too, the name her brainchild. She explains that the word *baido* stems from the Fourni islands she grew up on and refers to the time in the month when there is a full moon, and the two days either side of it. Traditionally, this was a time when the islanders wouldn't go out to fish because they could be seen by pirates – instead, they feasted and partied for all three days.

We take a seat outside, and soon Thodoris joins us. Marianthi brings wine, beer, water and sits with us to chat for a few moments, then takes our order. Several things on the menu aren't yet available as they're not in season. We put the menus aside and Marianthi tells us what *is* available. We order grilled meats, a fresh salad. Along with Urania's *koukia*, we will have enough to eat.

When the drinks arrive, we toast – to birthdays, to the upcoming summer season, and to *bioma*.

'What's *bioma*?' I ask.

'It literally means "life". But it implies more than that. It is the sum total of life's experience; it means to live life fully, passionately.'

I try the word out in my mouth. It suits the night, this experience, perfectly. It's cool on the terrace, the wind is rustling the vine above my head, the sea is now a dark mass in the distance and I'm surrounded by new friends.

Urania pulls out a package. In it is a soft cotton scarf in my favourite colours, red and white, interspersed with soft shades of pink. She's packed Ikarian olive oil soap within its folds. I put the scarf on, bring the soap to my nose, berate her – I did not ask her out to dinner so that she could bring me presents. She had done so much already.

Our food arrives, and Simone wanders up to join us, ordering herself some food too. The conversation turns to the small synchronicities and coincidences that seem to happen on the island. Someone stopping to give you a lift just when you need it; coming across a friend on the street you've just been thinking about; a work opportunity arising just when you want it the most.

Urania makes eye contact with Marianthi, who brings out homemade cake. On it is spelled out *Hronia Polla Spiri* in tiny chocolate buttons. '*Many years to you, Spiri*'.

Several days ago, I had not met Urania, or Thodoris, or Simone. I am touched and overwhelmed by their generosity, their thoughtfulness. Urania has given me considerate gifts, taken the time to make me a cake, come out with Thodoris after a long work day just so that I didn't have to celebrate my birthday alone.

As I blow out my candles, I think about generosity. Spirit. *Bioma*. I feel a strong sense of connection to these people and this place. I experience a heady feeling of having enough.

Leaving

Early the next morning, I run into Simone on the street as I am heading for a walk to Thea's to finally say goodbye to her. Simone invites me to a regular evening yoga class she runs with a small group of local women, held at the home of one of the participants, whose house is set atop a hill, several kilometres from the port town of Evdilos. As has been my inclination during this trip, I agree to go, wanting to take each opportunity that arises.

By the time I walk to Thea's place several kilometres away, the sun is high in the sky, the sea sparkling azure blue. I am tempted to veer off the path, to make my way across the rocks and immerse myself in the Aegean one more time – but I hold back, my more sensible self not willing to take the risk of slipping on the wet rocky path, or even drowning in this isolated, turbulent stretch. I've made it this far. I am now just days away from returning to my family.

Outside Thea's Inn, I run into Ilias. He makes me promise that if I ever turn my interest in Ikaria into a book, I will mention him. He jokes that I should write that he hunts wild goats in the middle of the night and always walks around splattered in blood.

Inside, I meet Thea and we sit down and talk more about the longevity phenomenon on the island. Thea believes it isn't helpful to be anxious about every little thing you eat or measure every little step you make. She is not at all surprised I have had such a good experience on the island, as I am good to people, so they too are good to me. I remember Kirios Nikos saying, 'If we have love inside us, we can send it out.'

Theia tells me to stay in touch, that she doesn't really want to say goodbye, as she knows this won't be the last time I visit the island. As we embrace, she leaves me with something her philosopher husband has said. 'The answer to a longer life is quite simple: "If you add life to your years, the years will come to you."'

—

Later that evening, as Simone and I are driving up the mountain to her class, she talks more about her belief in using yoga and meditation to work towards connecting the body with the soul, about helping participants move away from their brain and down into their hearts, into their bellies.

As we speak, Simone talks more about how she came to all this. She tells me she was in a serious accident some years ago. There is a palpable sadness in her voice when she talks of this time, her grief still teetering just below the surface, and I get the feeling her accident may have wiped out her promising career. She speaks about how she used the practice of mindfulness to help her rebuild her body, her heart, her life. She adds that living on the island has really helped.

After nearly two weeks on the island, what Simone is saying makes complete sense. I've allowed the island to lead me, each day, heading out to do one thing, and finding myself doing another. Tonight, once again, I feel I am in the right place.

As we take yoga mats and blankets out of the car, Simone refuses to accept payment for the class, saying that it is a gift for my birthday. On the terraza, I follow the yoga moves as best I can. Simone commends me on listening to my body so well, taking each yoga move only as far as I can, knowing my limitations. I realise I've become better at looking after myself in recent times.

I ponder how far I've come since the doctor's visit some years ago, less anxious about doing things right compared to others, more focused on doing them right for my own needs, for what my body tells me.

As the music plays, Simone talks us gently through a meditation to finish the session. Meanwhile, the elderly woman in the whitewashed house behind us is talking to a neighbour about the price of tomatoes, the evening news a backdrop to her lament. A dog nearby scratches the earth, a goat bleats and a scooter interrupts the rustle of wind through olive trees.

I lay still on my yoga mat, my mind calm. Every now and then I open my eyes to see if the sun has set, raise my head just a little. But mostly, I let Simone's words wash over me, and try to feel them in my body rather than in my head.

'Now you are sinking into the island, you are becoming Ikaria, you are letting the island, mother earth herself embrace you ...'

I hear the neighbour across the path leave. I follow her gaze in my mind, wonder what she makes of five women laying on bright mats, covered in blankets, listening to soft tribal beats. No doubt she will peg us as tourists or foreigners, though three of the women in the group are Greek and live on the island. They are the new generation of Greeks, who are taking something from their forebears and making it their own in the best way they know how, just as I am.

—

The next day, as I get ready to leave Ikaria, I take a final look at the sea from my balcony, and make an omelette with the last of my eggs, adding spinach and *Kathoura* cheese. Then I carefully wrap my gifts of local honey and homemade marmalades into my clothes. I go to the sweet shop downstairs to pay for my room and buy a bottle of cognac to give to Urania and Thodoris. I realise as I chat with the elderly owner that even she has made me feel at home. I'm sad to be leaving Ikaria, but I know that it's time to go home to my family, to my everyday life.

Urania takes me to the airport along with a few other passengers who are flying out. As we wind through the mountains, I say goodbye to the trees and the sea and the rocks and smile at how much the island has given me after only two short weeks.

I have learnt so many things since 'meeting' Stamatis Moraitis in the *New York Times* article. I've come out the other end eating more simply and cleanly most of the time. I feel more generous and spontaneous, more alive. I've become more social again, have more energy to do the things that are important to me. I've become more curious, more engaged with what is going on around me. And I've learnt to be kind to myself when I don't always meet my own high expectations.

More and more I'm thinking that the answers I was seeking are not just about living longer, but about living better each day, as mindfully and as lovingly as possible. As we drive along, I silently thank the island and its people for giving me so much.

Returning

On the flight back to Australia I feel completely relaxed. As well as visiting beloved Greek relatives, I finally made it to the fantastical Ikaria, 'filling my cup' physically and spiritually. I am ready to return home.

George, Dolores, Emmanuel, Mum and Dennis are waiting for me at the airport. I hug the kids first, tears rising unbidden to my eyes; I hold onto each of them long and hard. I kiss George firmly on the lips and hug him tight. My mother watches us, her look saying, 'See, this is what *really* matters.' There is a palpable sense of relief in her eyes that I have made it back. I wrap my arms around her and squeeze her tight too, relieved that nothing bad has happened to her while I've been away. I kiss Dennis on both cheeks. I am delirious. It feels as if I've been gone for years.

We make our way out into the cold winter night to the car, talking non-stop, catching up on the snippets of news it was hard to convey during our brief Skype conversations with their erratic internet connections.

At home, I am greeted with the aroma of baked food. George has made *ross il-forn*, his signature Maltese rice and beef dish. Mum has brought a pot of chicken soup and a tray of *pasticcio*. The house is light, warm and impeccably neat; the kitchen bench and sideboard dotted with vases of flowers. I smile, grateful to my family for stoking the home fires in my absence. How could I ever have doubted them?

We sit together around the table, the familiar lilt of conversation in Greek and English washing over me. I am struck once again by how good it is to be home.

Mum and Dennis soon leave and the kids slowly get ready for bed. I have a shower and join George in bed, where we hold each other tight and don't let go.

'We managed. But we really missed you. Like *really missed* you,' says George, his voice catching with emotion.

I hold him even tighter and say, 'You seem to have managed beautifully. I'm home now. Safe and sound. And I'm here to stay.'

We talk well into the night and then I hear his breathing settle into sleep. I lie awake a little longer, aware of my own breath, the faint beat of my heart, the heaviness of my limbs as they sink into our warm bed. I mould myself into George's sleeping back, and as my eyelids close I think, *this is more than enough.*

—

I've been back home several weeks now, and winter has settled in again. The lawn is wet and muddy, the fruit tree branches stark in the waning evening light. I'm enjoying transforming George's autumn pumpkins into winter soup; baking the last of the quinces into warming breakfasts. I've quickly taken my place back in the rhythms of family life and have returned to work.

My book club reconvenes and we're in the study discussing Ben Lawrence's *City of Thorns*, a book about the world's biggest refugee camp. Only Jill, a self-confessed book nerd, has read it to completion. Georgia, who recommended it, is absent; she's just come home from surgery and needs to be with her family. I'm halfway through the book, slowly reading the stories of nine people who have been thrown together in a dusty, tent-strewn town in Kenya's Dadaab. It's a challenging read, taking me uncomfortably away from the cosy confines of my own life. I don't want to rush through it in my usual fashion. The author has invested several years of his life to make sure these stories are told; I want to honour his effort, honour the experiences of those in the book.

The electric heater is on, and soft music is playing. There are three bottles of wine on the desk behind me, cheese and crackers on the table in front, a bowl of strawberries. I've made an orange, almond and semolina 'halva' cake from ingredients I had to hand so I wouldn't have to head out to the shops today.

My fellow book clubbers are all seated. I've just finished pouring them wine and am poised to pour myself a glass.

'So, what *is* the secret to long life?' Sarah-Jane asks in her characteristically forthright manner.

'I don't know that there is *one* secret ...' I reply, causing Sarah-Jane's shoulders to slump a little. It's not what she wants to hear.

'Okay, just let me sit down and I'll tell you ...' I take a breath and get ready to divulge the secrets to having a long, enjoyable life in a few pithy sentences, to summarise my last three years of yearning, learning and travelling to learn about longevity.

'If I had to say one thing, it would be that we need to keep moving everything, as often as we can for as long as possible – and in a way that is as natural and pleasurable as possible. I mean keep moving your body, your brain, your gut, even your sexy bits if you can ...'

I tell them the story of 95-year-old Nikos propositioning me so smoothly and subtly that I'm still not sure if it was for marriage or sex. Everyone laughs.

'And it's also important to have a strong sense of purpose,' I continue. 'I saw older people getting involved, giving advice, talking to young people, helping out. Even if they couldn't do things as fast as young people, they were still out there ...'

Heather nods. She has her very elderly mother over each weekend and gives her things to do so she can keep being active.

'We need to keep exercising our social skills too – find ways to keep getting out there, talking and connecting without having to think about it. I love that in my uncle's street someone had installed a park bench where neighbours congregated each night.'

'I've seen retired Italian and Greek men do the same thing at my local shopping mall,' says Leah.

'Yes, I've seen elderly Chinese men congregating at my local shopping centre. That's got to be a good thing. And there's something about the need to exercise our generosity, our giving impulse. It doesn't have to be about donating money; it might be giving your time, simply considering someone's needs, cooking something to share. Despite the difficult economic situation in Greece, so many people I met showed *filotimo*, an elusive word that is hard to translate but roughly means generosity to others.

'I believe older Ikarians survive longer because they ate, and still eat, so much plant food. And they eat less overall than we do here – there's so much research to suggest that eating moderately can help us live longer, with fewer chronic diseases. So many older islanders experienced hunger as children. They seem to sit down to one big, social meal a day. The other meals are small, and snacking is relatively absent.'

I refill glasses. Heather breaks open a packet of crisps. I reflect that while I'm eating less than I was three years ago, it's still a challenge to eat moderately, to stop when I am nearly full, particularly when I'm faced with my Achilles heel – salty chips.

'And then there's how we respond to stress. I met a lot of Ikarians who work hard; but they have a different attitude to time, seemingly making the most of each moment, appearing to live more in the present.'

Leah asks if it's hard to be back.

'I'm glad to be back. I really missed my family – and it felt like the right time to return. I'm trying to maintain something of the more relaxed, communal mindset in my days. My lists now are quite small, and they often include ringing people, moving, taking a bit of time out. And I've resigned myself that I'm probably going to put more loads of washing on than I will have hot breakfasts in my lifetime – thankfully George has continued to contribute since I've been back. I try and look at housework slightly differently now – it keeps me active, gives me a chance to think and daydream.'

We talk about the desire to have a long life. We agree that while it's probably a natural human instinct to want to live longer, it's best if most of that time can be spent feeling useful, having a sense that we are valued, that we can still contribute; and to have a good enough level of health to be able to enjoy the time.

'I did find that my questions naturally started evolving from talking about what leads to a *long* life to what leads to a *good* life.'

I look around. We are all women in our late forties or early fifties. We are all doing our best to raise families, balance work, look after ageing parents, and keep body and soul together as we navigate the day-to-day business of living. Who knows which of us will be here in thirty or forty years' time? I feel grateful that we are here now, connecting, talking, laughing.

After I see the women off, my eye canvasses the back wall of our study, which is lined with several floor-to-ceiling bookshelves filled with a messy array of books and knickknacks collected over a lifetime. My gaze stops at a small display of photos of Katerina cuddling much smaller versions of our children, their eyes squeezed shut with pleasure; Katerina and I doing a Greek dance in the forest; Katerina looking wistful in the last few weeks of her life. I silently tell her the latest.

The kids are growing up, Katerina mou; they're keeping me on my toes, as they should. You would be proud of them. And I'm doing okay too; still creating, still cooking, still engaging with my life as best I can each day. I'm still trying to tame my restless spirit, still trying to let go of things that don't really matter in the bigger scheme of things. You've left a wonderful legacy; you remind me not to rush through things, not worry too much about the future, to try to enjoy each moment.

I'm getting sleepy now. It's time to rest.
I love you.

I blow her a goodnight kiss and lock the door behind me.

Your
Ikaria

Have purpose

understand your purpose

How can we better understand and honour our purpose in life? Why do we get up in the morning? What drives us to keep going?

Exercise
Think about and then write down your answers to the following questions:

- What and who is most important to me?

- What gives me real joy and satisfaction?

- If I think back to a moment of grace in my life, what image first springs to mind?

- What would I like people to remember me for?

- If I knew I was going to die next week, what sorts of things would I prioritise this week?

Some of these questions are challenging. It might take you time to answer them. You might think about them and put them aside. Or the answers might come to you in a flash. Put down the words that come into your head, as I did with my 'purpose list'.

Honour your purpose

So often, we know what we should do to make changes in our lives, but we feel stuck in a rut, make excuses or simply ignore things because it feels too hard to muster the energy to transform our lives.

In my experience, change that is incremental and undertaken over time is most likely to last.

You don't need to make radical changes like quitting your job and joining an ashram (although you can if you want to). You might decide you want to work towards spending more time with your kids or an ageing parent. You might want to feel more energetic so you can do the things that mean the most to you. You might want a job that gives you more joy (but still helps you pay off the mortgage)! Or you might decide that you want to give back to your community now that you have the time and space in your life to do so.

Exercise

Sit down with pen and paper, and write down everything you can think of in answer to the following questions:

- What changes do I want to make in my life?

- Realistically, what changes can I make today / this week / this month / this year?

- Choose one change you'd like to make (for example, making more time for your family, quit smoking, etc.) and note what you need to do to make it.

Break the changes you want to make into bite-sized tasks that you can put on a list and tick off as you complete them (yes, yet another list – but this one is important!).

Befriend time

DON'T DO TOO MUCH

I still struggle with my impulse to do too much each day. If there is a spare moment, I will try to fill it with something – an exercise session, a social commitment, a phone call. Both my mother and I find it hard to relax. I envy my husband, who doesn't feel guilty taking time out during the day to do something relaxing for a few hours, like read a book.

The Ikarians I met get stressed, work hard and experience problems – but many of their rituals, such as walking, socialising and taking naps, help to dispel their stress.

Tips

- Try to do more things that are in keeping with your purpose and are important to you, and fewer activities which sap your energy and aren't in keeping with what is important.

- Practise saying no to activities that aren't important, without feeling guilty.

- Get into your body and out of your brain by walking, running, dancing, boxing, swimming, going to a yoga class, meditating, cooking, doing housework or any other activity that makes you feel good and that you can build into your life without causing more stress.

- Establish social rituals that help you deal with stress, whether it be a weekly walk with someone whose company you enjoy, a daily phone chat, a cuddle with your partner or kids at the end of the night, joining a club, volunteering for a charity, catching up with friends or other activities that help you relax and feel more fulfilled.

make peace with time

The ageing process is natural – we can't do in our forties what we did in our twenties. In some ways, getting older is a process of reconciling ourselves to loss – loss of capacity in our bodies, loss of youthful dreams and hopes, loss of time as it ticks away, loss of friends and family members who die. On the other hand, so many people I've met in recent years wear their elder wisdom with grace and dignity. The Ikarians were a real inspiration in this way. They spend time with young people and offer valuable skills and support to their families and villages. They are still able to offer meaningfully of themselves.

Life is finite. Time is finite. If we can live life as mindfully and fully as possible every single day, no matter our age, then I believe that's the best we can do.

reflect on what is 'enough'

Material things don't always plug the holes in your life. There is solid evidence that rising incomes do not correlate with higher levels of happiness. In fact, our aspirational spending can create some decent-sized holes as we get into more and more debt to feed our ever-expanding lifestyles and waistlines.

Contrary to what we are often led to believe, we can't (and perhaps shouldn't) have it all. Thinking we can makes us feel dissatisfied with our lives. We can't have the well-paying and satisfying career, the well-tended home, the well-behaved family, the interesting friends, the paid-off mortgage and a heap of leisure to boot. Life can be messy. It's often hard work. And sometimes it's confusing. But ultimately, it's worth living, and, I believe, it's worth living *well*.

Cook, eat, celebrate

eat FOOD THAT yiayia WOULD recognise

If you don't recognise an ingredient or a product, or it doesn't instinctively feel like real food, avoid putting it in your mouth, pantry or fridge.

Below are some quick and simple suggestions for how you can purchase and prepare more *yiayia*-friendly foods.

Breakfast

Non-yiayia foods	Yiayia alternatives
• Most breakfast cereals	• Oats prepared as porridge in winter or Bircher muesli in summer
• Breakfast biscuits	
• White bread toast with commercially bought spreads	• Eggs with a side of greens/tomatoes/avocado on grain toast
	• Unsweetened yoghurt with fruit and nuts
	• Wholegrain breads with natural spreads such as avocado, nut paste or tahini, or a drizzle of olive oil
	• Dinner leftovers (breakfast doesn't have to be sweet or include bread!)

Lunch/dinner

Non-yiayia foods

- Pre-prepared lasagne/ pizza/frozen meals and snacks
- Canned soups/meals
- Meats and poultry marinated in pre-prepared sauces
- Sandwiches/rolls with processed meats/ cheeses/spreads

Yiayia alternatives

- Wholegrain pasta, couscous and rice
- Whole cuts of meat and fish
- Fresh and frozen vegetables
- Soups made from homemade stock
- Beans and pulses
- Wholegrain bread sandwiches with natural spreads, salad vegetables and home-cooked meat or beans and pulses

Desserts/sweets/savoury snacks

Non-yiayia foods

- Flavoured yoghurt
- Ice-cream and flavoured ices
- Sweet pastries and biscuits, including croissants, donuts and muffins
- Potato crisps
- Savoury biscuits and rice crackers
- Commercial popping corn

Yiayia alternatives

- Unflavoured/ unsweetened yoghurt
- Whole fresh fruit
- Unsalted/unflavoured nuts (preferably still in the husk) and seeds
- Grain breads with natural toppings as above
- Whole corn kernels popped in olive oil

Flavouring/Sauces

Non-yiayia foods
- Commercially prepared sauces and flavourings

Yiayia alternatives
- Home-made tomato sauce
- Fresh and dried herbs and spices
- Lemon juice, vinegar
- Olive oil

Drinks

Non-yiayia foods
- Soft drinks (both sugar and artificially sweetened varieties)
- Fruit juices and drinks
- Flavoured teas
- Sweetened mineral waters

Yiayia alternatives
- Water, water and more water
- Herbal teas you make yourself from dried or fresh tea leaves
- Coffee

EAT FOOD YOU'VE COOKED YOURSELF AS MUCH AS POSSIBLE

We are spending an ever-increasing amount of our incomes on eating out. Collectively, Australians make 51.5 million visits to fast-food restaurants every month. As a result, it's become very easy for us to consume many calories in a short amount of time. That's a lot of added salts, sugars and dubious fats coming at us in large servings, which we have expended absolutely zero energy in preparing. Below are some tips for eating out to make it as healthy an experience as possible, as well as ways to help you eat more food you have prepared yourself.

Eat like a pauper when you dine out

- Order an entrée serve.

- Say no to upsizing food and drinks, no matter how good the deal seems.

- Choose water to accompany your meal. If drinking alcohol, intersperse this with water drinks.

- Order meals accompanied by as many plant foods as possible, such as sides of salads and vegetables, and small serves of protein such as eggs, fish or beans and legumes.

- Avoid fried foods, processed meats and bread-like products where possible.

- If ordering a desert, share it with someone.

- Eat slowly and enjoy your meal. Focus on the social aspects of eating and talking with others. Make it last.

Eating 'take out' when staying in – our top 'Friday nighters'
In our house, we tend to feel the greatest temptation to buy take-away food on Friday nights. These days I try to resist the urge for takeaway and prepare a nutritious meal instead.

The meal suggestions below take less time to cook than to order and pick up takeaway food. They can be cobbled together from things we generally have hanging around our fridge or pantry at the end of the week. Each cost less than $15 to $20 to feed a group of four and they won't give you indigestion. Use the money you save to go to the movies, give to charity or put it in a jar over a year so you can treat yourself to a holiday. If you spend $50 a week on takeaway, that's a saving of $2600 a year.

1. Eggs fried in a little olive oil with crumbled feta (optional) on grain toast. Serve with a side of vegetables (for example, panfried tomatoes and asparagus, steamed peas, corn or whatever else is in the freezer, vegetable crisper or garden).

2. Chickpeas in homemade tomato sauce with couscous and steamed greens.

3. Toasted pita bread filled with legume salad, a dollop of garlicky yoghurt and a pinch of chilli.

4. Filleted fish, pan fried in olive oil, along with seasonal vegetables (asparagus, chopped tomatoes, mushrooms, silverbeet, etc) seasoned with herbs of your choice and finished with a squeeze of lemon juice and chilli flakes.

5. Crusty grain bread with crumbled feta, tomato, olive oil and oregano.

6. Salad vegetables such as carrot, cucumber and celery dipped in tzatziki made from Greek yoghurt, olive oil, garlic and cucumber. Accompany with some feta or other cheese, a few olives and slices of grain bread for a healthy Mediterranean TV dinner.

celebrate real foods – and eat them as much as you can

Foods that are seasonal, tasty and nutritious make up the bulk of Ikarian diets and 'peasant'-style diets in general. These consist predominately of fresh and preserved fruit and vegetables, beans and legumes, wholegrains, nuts and seeds. These are supplemented with moderate amounts of dairy, meat, fish and plant-based oils such as olive oil. Sweets are eaten in moderation, are traditionally home-made and tend to be consumed during celebrations rather than every day.

Eating 'real' foods that you've mostly cooked yourself, and in sensible amounts, should make you feel good and give you the energy to do what you need to do. Generally, these foods are good for your gut, your brain and your waistline.

The details of what you eat will vary according to your tastes, culture, budget, how much time you have available and whether you like to cook or not ... There are so many variables, which is why breaking foods down into those we shouldn't have (such as high calorie, high carbohydrate, high fat, etc) and should have (superfoods, proteins, etc) is so counterintuitive. Food is fuel. Food is comfort. Food is so bound up in celebration, culture and joy. The more we embrace delicious real food that makes our bodies feel good, the quicker we can get over our angst about it.

Tips
Below are some ways to celebrate and eat more real foods:

- Shop mostly in the outer isles of your supermarket where the fresh food is – fruit and vegetables, nuts, meat and dairy.

- Ignore the specials at the front of most
  supermarket aisles – these are generally cheap
  but nutritionally empty foods such as soft
  drinks, crisps, biscuits and chocolate.

- Find local providores to buy fresh fruit,
  vegetables, beans, nuts and seeds rather than
  buying them exclusively at a supermarket. The
  produce is generally fresher, has higher turnover,
  is more varied and is likely to be cheaper and so
  you are more likely to eat more of these things.
  Stock up on staples that keep well.

- Challenge yourself to try new ingredients
  when they are in season – if artichokes or
  pomegranates or beetroots are cheap and
  plentiful at your local greengrocer, buy them
  and search for a recipe online.

eat moderately most of the time

There is a time and place for stuffing your face with corn chips
lathered in sour cream and tomato salsa, devouring a family-sized
bar of milk chocolate and sculling a litre of your favourite soft
drink. However, it's best not to do so all the time, or even most
of the time. It's not the occasional excesses that are responsible
for our collective excess weight woes, or lead to associated health
problems. It's the things we eat and drink every day, such as soft
drinks, nutrient-poor high-calorie snacks, highly refined breads
and pastries, and highly processed food-like products with added
sugars, fats, salts and preservatives.

It's not just what we eat, but how much of it. One of the Blue

Zones communities, the Okinawans, recite a phrase before every meal: *hara hachi bu*. This reminds them to eat to when they are 80 per cent full, rather than stuffing themselves to the point of bursting. Smaller portion sizes remind them to be mindful when eating and pay attention to their bodies.

As a population, fat is creeping up on us insidiously, year after year. By and large, it's making us feel sluggish and sore. Eventually, it will likely make us sick. It's not our fault, but we owe it to ourselves to do something about it. Personally, I'm quite terrified of going into a nursing home and needing to be transported from my bed to a chair in a harness.

Tips

Below are some tips for eating moderately.

- Gradually decrease your portion sizes at each meal. For some people, using smaller plates helps.

- Serve food onto your plates away from the table.

- Avoid seconds. If still hungry after a meal, drink water and wait a little – it takes twenty minutes for your body to indicate fullness. If still hungry, add more 'filling' food to your plate, such as salad or vegetables.

- Learn to listen to your body – are you really hungry? Perhaps you are thirsty, or tired or stressed. So many of us partake in emotional eating. Perhaps you need a drink, or a rest, or to do something else constructive to distract you. If you feel you have an addiction to food or you have tried unsuccessfully over a long time to shed excess weight, get professional help – you don't have to do this on your own.

PLANT UP, ANIMAL DOWN

The traditional Ikarian diet is high in vegetables and fruits, beans, whole grains, potatoes and olive oil – and low in red meat.

Eating more plant food is good for the environment. It's also cheaper than eating meat, and better for our bodies. Data sourced from the UK-based Nurses' Health Study found that people who replace a small amount of animal proteins (particularly from red meat) with plant proteins can add years to their life.

Gradually adding more plant foods to your plate and your shopping list will make it easier to eat more without thinking about it too much. More than nine out of ten Australians don't eat the recommended amount of fruit and vegetables each day. Often, we lack imagination when we think about plant foods. They don't have to be a side of sad, tasteless steamed vegetables. They might be lima beans in homemade tomato sauce with garden herbs; a medley of baked vegetables in olive oil and garlic; or grilled courgettes and eggplants garnished with a dollop of yoghurt and paprika. These things don't take very long to prepare and are cheap and tasty. If possible, it's best to buy fruit and vegetables that are in season.

Tips

- Use meat as a flavouring or small addition to your meal rather than the main ingredient.

- Bulk meat stews up with vegetables and beans. Consider adding leafy greens (spinach, silverbeet, kale) to as many dishes as you can.

- Replace one meat dish with a bean/legume dish each week.

- Buy a small amount of dairy and meat products each week. Once you run out, don't buy them again until the following week.

DITCH GUILT

We live in a country where highly processed, takeaway and convenience foods are on every major shopping strip, on every screen, and at the end of every aisle in our supermarkets. So, when we're told to deprive ourselves of these things in the interest of good health, we often want to arc up like a hungry child in a lolly shop (or is that just me?). I believe our systems are hardwired to respond to our environments – and so in an environment of plenty, we instinctively consume.

Sometimes I feel like hot chips. Sometimes I crave Vegemite toast with butter. Sometimes I want to indulge in chocolate. But I know that if I eat these things all the time, my body will let me know about it. Over time, I know that eating these things too often will lead to me putting on weight, feeling sluggish and getting constipated. The pleasure of eating these things lasts for a few minutes, but the consequences last much longer. That knowledge helps me keep on track.

Most of the time, I eat foods that make me feel good. If I have treats, I make sure to really enjoy them. Statistics show that we are much less likely to make a change if we feel badly about the behaviour.

Why waste time on guilt? Life is too short.

CUT DOWN ON SNACKING

I tell my kids that the world won't stop if we don't have crisps or chocolate biscuits or cakes in the pantry. Around 96 per cent of Australians say they regularly consume snack foods, with chocolate up there as one of our first choices.

Tips

- Keep fruit, nuts and seeds handy at work or when you are out so you're not tempted to make a chocolate or sweet run at 3 pm each day.

- Avoid buying highly processed snacks – if they're not in your home, you're less likely to eat them.

- Store whole food snacks so they're clearly visible in your fridge and pantry, and carry some of these with you when out for longer periods so that you are not tempted by less healthy snacks.

- Learn to listen to your hunger cues – are you really feeling hungry, or simply tired, thirsty or emotionally flat and using food to fill the gap?

- Avoid getting overly hungry, which can result in you reaching for snacks when what you need is a proper meal.

MOSTLY DRINK WATER. DRINK TEA, COFFEE AND WINE IN MODERATION.

Soft drinks alone are adding to our collective waistlines, with US estimates showing that consuming one can of soft drink per day can lead to a 6.75-kilogram weight gain in one year. Nearly half of Australian children aged two to sixteen consume sugar sweetened beverages (including energy drinks) every day.

WHAT THE IKARIANS DO – AND WHY IT'S GOOD FOR YOU

Drink water

The Ikarian drink of choice is water. While sugary drinks have made inroads in recent decades, they are still a 'treat' drink rather than an everyday phenomenon. Avoid keeping soft drinks at home – if they aren't there to tempt you, you will be less likely to consume them.

Drink coffee

It is thought that the boiled Greek coffee that the Ikarians (and many Greeks) drink may be associated with good heart health. There is compelling research to suggest that coffee drinkers in general may increase their lifespan, and have lower risk of developing cancer of the liver, type 2 diabetes, and heart attacks.

Whatever coffee you drink, ensure that it is not loaded with sugar and sugar syrups (as in some takeaways or 'gourmet' versions). Drinking a lot of milk-based coffees over the course of the day can also add up to excess energy and thus weight gain.

Drink herbal teas

The Ikarians make a regular practice of drinking herbal teas made from local wild herbs, including chamomile, mint and other local herbs. Herbs such as these lower blood pressure, and decrease their risk of heart disease and dementia. Herbs have traditionally been used in dealing with everyday ailments such as stomach pains, headaches and insomnia. Consider adding unsweetened herbal teas to your list of drinks consumed each day.

Drink alcohol in moderation and in company

In Australia, one in five of us drink alcohol at dangerous levels. Dangerous drinking is simply the four or five drinks some of us may have at the pub on a Friday night, or at a family barbecue on a Sunday. This sort of drinking places us at lifetime risk (chance) of getting an alcohol-related disease or injury.

The Ikarians largely drink their own homemade wine, which is absent of nitrates and pesticides. They generally drink in social situations, and almost always with food.

While research varies, there is a potential link between moderate alcohol consumption and reduced dementia risk. Some studies have found that drinking wine in particular is good for heart health, commonly known as the 'French Paradox'. In the light of competing evidence, and not really wanting to give up alcohol completely, I find myself returning to the age-old Greek adage *pan metron ariston* – everything in moderation.

Whatever your drink of choice, consider drinking water between drinks, make it a practice to drink mostly in company, and ensure you have a few alcohol-free days each week. If you are trying to manage your weight, remember that alcohol is dense in energy but lacking in nutrition – and I speak from experience when I say that you may be inclined to eat more while you are drinking.

Move, rest and relax

The Ikarians live in mountain and seaside villages that compel them to move all the time. Their day-to-day life requires vigorous walking, tending of terraced gardens and looking after livestock. They move without thinking about it.

Here in Australia and similar countries such as the US and the UK, we sit down too much and don't move enough. Australians spend as much as 80 per cent of our working day sedentary. A joint study by the Australian National University and the University of Sydney found that those who sat for eight hours a day (which is most of us who work in offices) have a 15 per cent greater risk of early death than those who move more. Even those who exercised regularly risked shortening their lifespan if most of their daily hours were sedentary. A University of Queensland study calculated that for every hour of (seated) TV watching, a person over the age of twenty-five cuts about twenty-two minutes from their lifespan.

embrace everyday movement

Much as I have a vexed relationship with housework (why can't everything just *stay clean*?), I understand now that the work we do around our homes and gardens keeps us moving. Having a neat home makes me feel good, just as maintaining a prolific garden satisfies my partner. I now make my housework more active – making several trips to the clothesline rather than trying to lug a few loads of washing out in one go.

The main change I've made to increase how much I move around is to take the train to work – come rain, hail or shine. I've added three kilometres of steps to my day, without even really noticing it. This means I don't have to worry about parking around the busy campus where I work, and I have some 'thinking' time as I walk to and from work rather than trying to negotiate traffic. On the days I work, I generally amass 10,000 steps by mid-afternoon. When I have time, on my way home I get off the train a few stops early and hit my goal of 10,000 steps even more quickly. Overall, I am more energetic, feel nicely tired at the end of the night, I sleep better and wake up with more energy.

Channel the Ikarians and do as much incidental exercise as you can each day – below are some tips to get you started.

Tips

In the home

- Consider everyday tasks such as housework, gardening and home maintenance as a chance to move.

- Avoid purchasing automated devices that replace good old elbow grease – think leaf blowers, automatic juicing machines, and remote controls for just about everything.

- If you have shops nearby, walk rather than drive.

Outside the home

- Walk up escalators.

- Take the stairs rather than lifts.

- Stand rather than sit on public transport.

- Park your car a little further when shopping, going to work, picking up kids, etc.

- Avoid taking your car where possible for local trips.

In the workplace

- Put things you need to use regularly – the bin, your kettle, the printer – at a distance.

- Go and talk to colleagues instead of ringing or emailing them.

- Set a desktop timer to go off every 30 minutes to encourage you to stretch.

- Go for a five-minute powerwalk around the block every hour or two to increase the flow of oxygen to your brain, get some sun on your skin and move your limbs.

- Walk with colleagues at lunchtime, replace a meeting with a walk or hold standing meetings.

THERE'S STILL A PLACE FOR RIGOROUS EXERCISE

While I would like to ditch rigorous exercise, my sedentary job means I don't get enough. My daughter and I go to group fitness classes to increase our fitness, manage our weight and help with overall feelings of wellness.

Tips

- Choose exercise that you enjoy, such as dancing, running, swimming, or a team sport

- Make it easy on yourself. If the exercise you enjoy is free as well as easy to schedule, you are more likely to do it. Dance to tacky '80s pop clips, run, jog, do online exercise videos or whatever else takes your fancy. All you need to do is find 2 to 3 hours in your week to replace sedentary activities with more active ones. Given we are spending 12.5 hours per week on Facebook alone, it shouldn't be too hard to find the time to be more active.

- Make a commitment to a team sport or a regular class to help you stay on track.

- Make small, incremental changes and build on these over time.

LISTEN TO YOUR BODY

As my body has changed over time, I am unable to do some of the things I did as a young person. So often I see people at my gym pushing through injury to keep going with their fitness routines, but at the cost of pain and further injury. Others launch into very rigorous exercise after months or years of doing none. It is important to listen to your body and consider what it can and won't do.

- Listen to your body for tiredness cues – and honour these by sleeping more or resting.

- If you feel too tired to do rigorous exercise, replace this with a walk or another form of more gentle exercise.

- Pain is the body's way of indicating that something is not right – listen and honour that by considering what is causing the pain and ways that you might address it.

CONNECT WITH THOSE AROUND YOU THROUGH MOVEMENT

Tips

- Create regular movement rituals with someone else.

- Replace a coffee date with a walking date.

- Walk the dog if you have one – and take a neighbour, friend or family member with you.

247

GET ENOUGH SLEEP

Studies show that a minimum of seven hours of sleep a night is essential for optimal health for those aged eighteen to sixty. Sleep deprivation leads to tiredness, memory problems and lack of concentration, and is associated with depression and anxiety.

It is thought that the Ikarians' after-lunch siesta helps them to relax – it may be the reason for their low levels of depression. Getting the right amount of sleep will help you be more productive and relaxed and have more sustained energy. In her book *The Sleep Revolution*, Ariana Huffington likens sleep to 'bringing in the overnight cleaning crew to clear the toxic waste proteins that accumulate between brain cells during the day'.

Tips

- If you feel you have a lot to do, make a list and put it aside to do tomorrow. Nothing earthshaking will happen if you don't mop the floor or check those Facebook posts.

- Work backwards from the time you need to get up to ensure that you get the required amount of sleep. Half an hour before your designated bedtime, turn off all screens, darken your room, have a warm drink, and do something relaxing such as reading or a short meditation.

- Moving enough throughout your day, eating well and avoiding caffeinated drinks in the latter half of the day can help to set the scene for a better night's sleep.

- Avoid eating and drinking alcohol late at night.

Really connect

Our Western lifestyle makes it harder to form and maintain meaningful connections. Some studies have shown that rather than making us feel connected, online social media can contribute to loneliness and reduce overall life-satisfaction. The proportion of Australians experiencing loneliness in any given year is around one in ten people. Research that reviewed 148 studies on the matter concluded that loneliness is as harmful to our health as smoking fifteen cigarettes a day.

make time to connect with those who are important to you

The 2007 National Survey of Mental Health and Wellbeing found that one in five Australians aged sixteen to eighty-five experienced mental disorders in the previous year. This is equivalent to almost 3.2 million Australians. Social support, and particularly the emotional support from a close relationship, is one important protective factor for mental health problems.

Traditional 'village' structures tend to be few and far between in cities and towns, where we often live far from the people we grew up with, people who might have traditionally supported us as we grew our own families. So many of us are now working to support the sort of lifestyle we expect to have – mortgaging ourselves to the hilt to acquire homes, expensive phones and electronic entertainments – leaving less time to simply be with the people who are important to us.

Whomever you want to connect with, think about ways you can set things in place to do that. Prioritise meaningful connections, as these will keep you healthier and happier for longer.

Tips
Some simple rituals that can help you connect:

- Whether you live alone or with others, try to eat at the dinner table with family or friends as much as possible. If this is difficult because everyone has different commitments, agree on a night when it happens – and where everyone agrees that it's not negotiable.

- Wash and dry the dishes with the people you live with (even if you have a dishwasher!).

- Make a habit of taking an evening walk with someone when the weather is fine.

- If you have a partner, aim to have an impromptu and regular 'date' at home – where you cook a simple meal, set up candles and ask each other how you are. Listen to each other properly. Take time for each other over breakfast of a weekend (before your kids wake up if you have teenagers) or late at night over supper (if you have young and early risers).

- Set up a monthly dinner, a weekly walk, a daily
  phone call with someone you want to spend
  more time with – whatever works for you.
  Agree to commit to it and put it in your diary.
  If it doesn't work or stresses you out, review it.

- Help older people in your life connect with
  younger people, perhaps setting up Skype
  for a grandparent to read a nightly story to a
  grandchild who lives far away, or an aunt to
  teach a teenager a new skill.

Be Generous every Day

The everyday generosity that I experienced while on the island
of Ikaria was uplifting. From being offered food, to lifts, to company, it all helped me to feel welcome and connected to people
whom I had not previously met.

Generous people report being happier, healthier and more
satisfied with life than those who don't give. Personally, being
generous makes me feel that I am making a contribution and a
difference to the world, however small.

Generosity does not mean you need to give large amounts of
money to charity each year. It can be simple acts of generosity
each day: a smile to a stranger, delivering a meal to someone who
is unwell, volunteering your time to share a skill or passion.

Tips

- Consider what is going well in your life
  and what you are grateful for. Once you
  acknowledge what is going well, you are more
  likely to share your life with others.

- Consider what your skills and strengths are, and how you can share these meaningfully on a day-to-day basis – it might be cooking a meal for someone who is ill, helping someone with a job application or making a regular phone call to someone who would appreciate it.

- If you have time to volunteer your time, choose a cause that you feel strongly about and to which you feel you could make a meaningful contribution.

- Raise money for a cause connected with your passion – be it a charity or an inspirational person. Consider how you can help – organising a fundraiser with friends, doing a fun run, or making a donation.

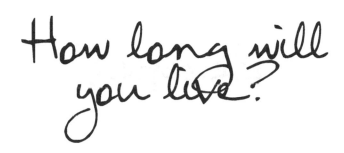
How long will you live?

The good folk at Blue Zones have developed two simple online tests to measure overall life expectancy and happiness.

Many such tests are available on the internet, but the Blue Zones ones are comprehensive and rigorous, but also easy and quick to complete. They are based on statistical probability – that is, they assess the things you do in your life and measure their likely effect on how long you might live.

Once you've done the tests, and put in place some of the tips in this book, do the tests again after a few months to see if you have improved your score.

True VITALITY TEST

This test calculates your life expectancy, how long you'll stay healthy and gives you personalised recommendation for getting the most good years out of life.

apps.bluezones.com/en/vitality/

True Happiness Test

This test, based on the leading scientific research into well-being, will help you improve your environment to maximise your happiness.

apps.bluezones.com/en/happiness

Recipes

stamatis family fava

Fava is a traditional staple food in Ikaria – it is cheap, filling and nourishing. Serve it as you would a cold soup. It is delicious accompanied by bread, olives and cheese.

INGREDIENTS

- 225g yellow split peas
- 1 medium brown onion, chopped
- 1 small clove garlic, crushed
- juice of ½ a lemon
- 1 teaspoon olive oil
- salt and black pepper, to taste
- paprika to garnish

METHOD

Pick over the split peas to remove any discoloured ones, and rinse. Place them in a large saucepan with the onions and enough water to cover. Bring to the boil, then reduce the heat and simmer for 30 to 45 minutes, until the split peas are thick and mushy. If there is still some water remaining, drain it off before transferring the peas to a bowl.

Beat in the garlic, lemon juice and oil until thick and well blended. Leave to cool, then add salt and pepper to taste and garnish with paprika.

Serves 4

Thea's soufiko
(Summer vegetable dish)

Soufiko is a traditional Ikarian vegetable dish which takes advantage of summer vegetables. It is quick, healthy, tasty and very versatile. Serve as a main course on its own, as a side dish, or over rice or pasta.

INGREDIENTS

- 2 eggplants, coarsely chopped
- 2 zucchinis, coarsely chopped
- 2 onions, cut in thick slices
- 3 garlic cloves, sliced
- 3 green or sweet red peppers, thinly sliced
- 4 tablespoons olive oil
- 1 large chopped tomato
- salt and black pepper, to taste
- fresh or dried oregano and olive oil to serve

METHOD

In a large frypan place the ingredients in the order that they are listed. Cover and cook on low heat for about 20 to 30 minutes, covered. Occasionally shake the pan gently (rather than using a spoon or spatula) so that it does not stick. The dish is ready when the vegetables are soft. Sprinkle a little oregano and olive oil on top, and serve immediately.

Serves 4

Ilia's baked chickpeas

Chickpeas are a staple of Ikarian cuisine and they now make a regular appearance on our table too. At least once a fortnight I cook a large batch and freeze most for use during the week, adding them to salad, stews, soups, curries and the kids' lunchboxes.

INGREDIENTS

- 500g dried chickpeas
- 2 medium carrots, peeled and quartered
- 2 small zucchinis, quartered
- 2 tablespoons fresh mint, chopped
- 2 tablespoons fresh dill, chopped
- 2 tablespoons fresh flatleaf parsley, chopped
- 2 medium onions, diced
- 2 small tomatoes, chopped
- 3 tablespoons olive oil (with extra to serve)
- salt, to taste

METHOD

Soak chickpeas overnight. Place in saucepan, cover with water and bring to a boil. Rinse and drain, then place once again in saucepan, cover with fresh water and boil until soft. Drain off, reserving a cup of the broth. Place the carrots and zucchinis in a baking dish, then layer with the herbs, onion, tomatoes and chickpeas. Add the cup of broth from the chickpeas, the olive oil and salt to taste. Cook uncovered in oven at 200°C. After approximately 15 minutes, or when the top is golden, mix and cook further until crisp on top. Drizzle with olive oil to serve.

Serves 4

spiri's silverbeet dolmathakia

Dolmathakia are traditionally made with fresh young leaves from a grapevine in the springtime. My *Theia* Kanella would collect these and place them tightly in a jar – inexplicably, they would keep for many months. You can buy leaves preserved in brine at most Greek delicatessens. I had *dolmathakia* several times while in Greece – and each time they were slightly different. Some are made with cabbage leaves and the addition of mince to the rice, others with a lemon and egg sauce. In the spirit of improvisation, I use silverbeet, which grows prolifically in our garden for a few months each year.

INGREDIENTS

- 20–30 silverbeet leaves (young, small leaves work best)
- 1 cup long grain rice, cooked
- 1 cup olive oil
- 2 medium onions, grated
- ½ cup parsley, chopped
- ¼ cup dill, chopped
- 1 tablespoon mint, chopped
- juice of 2 medium lemons
- salt and black pepper, to taste

METHOD

Wash silverbeet leaves and remove stalks. Allow to drain. Prepare the rice mixture by placing the rice, onions, herbs and half the olive oil in a bowl. Season with salt and pepper.

Take one silverbeet leaf at a time and place a tablespoon of the rice mixture a little in from the stalk end of the silverbeet. Carefully fold this over to cover the filling. If the stalk is too inflexible to roll, trim this back a little more and place the rice halfway along the leaf. Tuck in each side of the leaf and roll, continuing until the filling is enclosed tightly.

Carefully place your parcels in a shallow pot, until they are packed in snugly. Pour the remaining oil over them and then slowly pour 1 ½ cups of boiled water over them, along with the lemon juice. Place a plate upside down over the top to anchor the *dolmathakia* down. Cook for approximately 45 minutes to an hour on very low heat, or until rice is cooked through.

Enjoy as an entrée or main course, hot or cold.

Serves 4 as a main course

Chrysoula's pasticcio

This dish has comfort written all over it. It is quite rich and takes a little while to prepare. As such, it was traditionally made for special occasions – generally for Sunday lunch or to eat during a celebration. This recipe makes enough for four people to eat over several days, or it could be shared with a bigger group.

INGREDIENTS

For the meat sauce and pasta layers

- 2 tablespoons olive oil
- 1 kg good-quality lamb or beef mince
- 1 large onion, finely chopped
- 1 clove garlic, coarsely chopped
- 1 bay leaf
- 3 sprigs thyme
- 1 teaspoon oregano
- a few pinches of cinnamon
- 1 cup or can chopped tomatoes
- salt and black pepper, to taste
- 500g dried pasta (penne, macaroni or rigatoni work best)

For the béchamel sauce

- 100g butter
- 100g plain flour
- 1 litre whole milk
- ½ cup parmesan or cheddar cheese
- 2 eggs
- a pinch of grated nutmeg
- salt and black pepper, to taste

METHOD

Prepare a 30 × 20 × 4 cm baking dish (or close approximation) with a splash of olive oil or butter. Set aside.

Heat the oil and brown the mince, breaking it up into small pieces. Add the garlic, herbs, cinnamon and seasoning, and cook for a few minutes. Add the tomatoes and one cup of boiled water. Simmer on low heat for 45 minutes. Check every now and then to see that there is enough water; add more if it looks dry.

Boil pasta in salted water. When al dente (still a little firm but not chalky), drain and set aside.

Mix the cooked sauce through the pasta and transfer the mixture to the prepared baking dish.

For the béchamel sauce, heat the butter in a heavy-set saucepan or frypan. Add the flour to the butter and stir continuously for a few minutes until if forms a paste. Gradually add the milk, stirring the whole time, until you have a smooth sauce. Stir in the cheese and take off the heat.

Whisk the eggs lightly with the nutmeg and seasoning, and add to the mixture, stirring in.

Evenly pour the béchamel over the pasta mixture and smooth over with a spatula – you should not be able to see any of the pasta mixture. Bake in a moderate oven for approximately 30 to 40 minutes or until golden.

Serve with salad or a side of roasted or steamed vegetables.

Note: For a vegetarian version of this dish, replace the mince with eggplant and cook until soft. Add a can of drained brown lentils to the sauce in the last few minutes of the cooking process.

Serves 10–12

Fiona's quick spaghetti with pea and herb pesto

This recipe is quick to make, packed with life-giving herbs, olive oil and garlic, and tastes delicious – what's there not to like?

INGREDIENTS

- 500g spaghetti
- 1 cup frozen or fresh peas
- 2 cloves garlic, peeled
- ¼ cup lightly toasted pine nuts
- ½ cup lightly packed fresh basil leaves
- ¼ cup lightly packed fresh mint leaves
- ½ cup flakes parmesan cheese
- 2 tablespoons extra virgin olive oil
- salt and black pepper, to taste

METHOD

Cook pasta in boiling salted water. Cook peas until tender. Allow peas to cool and transfer to a food processor with the garlic, pine nuts, herbs, cheese, oil, salt and pepper. Process until smooth. Toss pea mixture through hot pasta. Serve with extra parmesan. (And crusty bread goes down well too!)

Serves 4

Spiri's orange, almond and semolina cake

A version of this recipe was given to me by a family friend many years ago. It is my 'go to' recipe when I want to make a cake for any occasion. It tastes best with oranges that are in season – preferably plucked straight off the tree if you have that luxury. Generally, I have the other ingredients in my pantry. Coarse semolina is getting harder to find, but most Mediterranean and Middle Eastern food shops stock it.

INGREDIENTS

For the cake

- 1 cup olive oil
- ¾ cup caster sugar
- 4 teaspoons orange rind
- 4 eggs
- 2 cups almond meal
- 2 teaspoons baking powder (gluten-free version available)
- 2 cups (coarse) semolina (or replace with fine polenta for a gluten-free version)
- 2 tablespoons freshly squeezed orange juice

For the syrup

- 1 cup caster sugar
- 2 cups freshly squeezed orange juice
- 2 tablespoons brandy or Grand Marnier (optional)
- extra orange peel, julienned (optional)

METHOD

Preheat oven to 200°C and prepare a round baking pan (approximately 20cm) with olive oil or baking paper to stop the cake from sticking to the tin.

Mix oil, sugar and orange rind together with an electric beater until light and fluffy. Add eggs one at a time while continuing to beat.

Add half the dry ingredients (almond meal, baking powder and semolina) and half the orange juice, mix, and then add the remaining ingredients. The mixture should be quite sticky and firm, a little like a biscuit mixture.

Transfer to prepared baking pan and bake for approximately 40 to 45 minutes. Insert a skewer, and if it comes out clean, it is ready. The cake should be a lovely golden colour.

While the cake is baking, pour two cups of orange juice into a saucepan with one cup caster sugar. If you like, you can add orange peel julienned into very thin strips. Stir until sugar is dissolved. Once dissolved, bring to the boil and reduce heat. Allow to simmer for five minutes or so, without stirring. Add Grand Marnier if using.

When cake has cooled slightly in its tin, turn it out into a larger oven-proof dish with lips around the side (to 'catch' the syrup). Pour over half the prepared syrup and return to the oven for 5 minutes. Pour over the remaining syrup and let steep. When cooled, serve as is, or with ice-cream or thick cream.

Serves 12

Acknowledgements

First thanks go to my agent Jacinta di Mase, who got behind the idea of this book and didn't give up on it, or me. To Caitlin Yates, Kirstie Innes-Will and the talented team at Nero, thanks for your amazing support, and for trusting that this was an important story to tell. Thanks also to Louise Thurtell, editor extraordinaire, who worked her magic on my words. Without these people, *My Ikaria* would never have seen the light of day.

To the writers who make up my creative village – Jacqueline Ross, Jane Woollard, Maryrose Cuskelly, Myfanwy Jones, Nicolas Brasch, Sam Lawry, Tess Woods and Wendy Meddings – I am indebted to you for your unfailing encouragement, patience and support.

Thank you to the people in Ikaria who were so generous with their time and spirit, particularly Gayle Winegar, Ilias and Thea Parikos, Isabelle Bachmann, Niki and Stella Tsakalou, 'Pappou' Nikolaos Kastanias, Simone Leona Hueber, Thodoris Koukoumtzis, and Urania Mytika. A special thanks to my Melbourne-based Ikarian friends Dorothy and Lisa Kastanias, and Sotiris and Vaso Kamitsis.

To Alexis Tellis and Angela Elbarbar for your passion when it comes to all things Greek, and to Fiona Pirperis for the walks, talks and sharing of recipes.

In so many ways, this book is a celebration of all the people in my life who make it meaningful each day. To my extended family both here and in Greece, and to my husband's family – this is as good a time as any to say thank you for all that you do. Special thanks go to my in-laws Dolores and Alfred Mifsud, my cousin Kathy Petras, my brother Dennis Tsintziras, my mother Chrysoula Tsintziras, my husband George Mifsud, and our children, Dolores and Emmanuel Mifsud.

CPSIA information can be obtained
at www.ICGtesting.com
Printed in the USA
BVHW031112100223
658204BV00007B/849